CRITICAL ESSAYS ON

Editors:
Linda Cookson
Bryan Loughrey

LONGMAN
LITERATURE
GUIDES

Longman Literature Guides

Editors: Linda Cookson and Bryan Loughrey

Titles in the series:

CONTENTS

PREFACE

Like all professional groups, literary critics have developed their own specialised language. This is not necessarily a bad thing. Sometimes complex concepts can only be described in a terminology far removed from everyday speech. Academic jargon, however, creates an unnecessary barrier between the critic and the intelligent but less practised reader.

This danger is particularly acute where scholarly books and articles are re-packaged for a student audience. Critical anthologies, for example, often contain extracts from longer studies originally written for specialists. Deprived of their original context, these passages can puzzle and at times mislead. The essays in this volume, however, are all specially commissioned, self-contained works, written with the needs of students firmly in mind.

This is not to say that the contributors — all experienced critics and teachers — have in any way attempted to simplify the complexity of the issues with which they deal. On the contrary, they explore the central problems of the text from a variety of critical perspectives, reaching conclusions which are challenging and at times mutually contradictory.

They try, however, to present their arguments in a direct, accessible language and to work within the limitations of scope and length which students inevitably face. For this reason, essays are generally rather briefer than is the practice; they address quite specific topics; and, in line with examination requirements, they incorporate precise textual detail into the body of the discussion.

They offer, therefore, working examples of the kind of essay-writing skills which students themselves are expected to develop. Their diversity, however, should act as a reminder that in the field of literary studies there is no such thing as a 'model' answer. Good essays are the outcome of a creative engagement with literature, of sensitive, attentive reading and careful thought. We hope that those contained in this volume will encourage students to return to the most important starting point of all, the text itself, with renewed excitement and the determination to explore more fully their own critical responses.

How to use this volume

Obviously enough, you should start by reading the text in question. The one assumption that all the contributors make is that you are already familiar with this. It would be helpful, of course, to have read further — perhaps other works by the same author or by influential contemporaries. But we don't assume that you have yet had the opportunity to do this and any references to historical background or to other works of literature are explained.

You should, perhaps, have a few things to hand. It is always a good idea to keep a copy of the text nearby when reading critical studies. You will almost certainly want to consult it when checking the context of quotations or pausing to consider the validity of the critic's interpretation. You should also try to have access to a good dictionary, and ideally a copy of a dictionary of literary terms as well. The contributors have tried to avoid jargon and to express themselves clearly and directly. But inevitably there will be occasional words or phrases with which you are unfamiliar. Finally, we would encourage you to make notes, summarising not just the argument of each essay but also your own responses to what you have read. So keep a pencil and notebook at the ready.

Suitably equipped, the best thing to do is simply begin with whichever topic most interests you. We have deliberately organised each volume so that the essays may be read in any order. One consequence of this is that, for the sake of clarity and self-containment, there is occasionally a degree of overlap between essays. But at least you are not forced to follow one — fairly arbitrary — reading sequence.

Each essay is followed by brief 'Afterthoughts', designed to highlight points of critical interest. But remember, these are only there to remind you that it is *your* responsibility to question what you read. The essays printed here are not a series of 'model' answers to be slavishly imitated and in no way should they be regarded as anything other than a guide or stimulus for your own thinking. We hope for a critically involved response: 'That was interesting. But if *I* were tackling the topic . . .!'

Read the essays in this spirit and you'll pick up many of the skills of critical composition in the process. We have, however, tried to provide more explicit advice in 'A practical guide to essay writing'. You may find this helpful, but do not imagine it offers any magic formulas. The quality of your essays ultimately depends on the quality of your engagement with literary texts. We hope this volume spurs you on to read these with greater understanding and to explore your responses in greater depth.

Cedric Watts

Cedric Watts is Professor of English at Sussex University, and author of numerous scholarly publications.

ESSAY

Keatsian thresholds

1

Your thumb-print is unique: nobody else has a thumb-print exactly like it. Third-rate writers are so conventional and derivative that their writings are virtually interchangeable; but the works of first-rate writers are original and distinctive, marked by the individual's own imaginative thumb-print. If I asked a teacher to describe Keats's particular 'thumb-print', the teacher would probably give a reply like this: 'It's Keats's sensuousness, of course: his love of an aptly rich diction for conveying the sensuous pleasures of life. You only have to recall the opening of his ode "To Autumn" in order to feel the strength of that preoccupation:

> Season of mists and mellow fruitfulness,
>   Close bosom-friend of the maturing sun;
> Conspiring with him how to load and bless
>   With fruit the vines that round the thatch-eaves run;
> To bend with apples the moss'd cottage-trees,
>   And fill all fruit with ripeness to the core;
>   To swell the gourd, and plump the hazel shells
>   With a sweet kernel . . .

The lines not only recall the richness of nature; they also, because of their fullness of sound-patterning (alliteration and assonance) increase the richness of language itself; and consequently, there's a characteristic Keatsian harmony between the sensuous things described and the sensousness of the describing language.' That's what a teacher might rightly say. But it seems to me that Keats also has another kind of imaginative thumbprint, and one which is much less commonly identified. Keats is the poet of thresholds and threshold-states.

Whether you look at his letters or his long poems or his short poems, you find that Keats is again and again preoccupied with thresholds of one kind or another. Let's look first at two of the most famous passages in his letters.

> I compare human life to a large Mansion of Many Apartments ... The first we step into we call the infant or thoughtless Chamber ... but are at length imperceptibly impelled by the awakening of the thinking principle — within us — we no sooner get into the second Chamber, which I shall call the Chamber of Maiden-Thought, than we become intoxicated with the light and the atmosphere, we see nothing but pleasant wonders, and think of delaying there for ever in delight: However among the effects this breathing is father of is that tremendous one of sharpening one's vision into the heart and nature of Man — of convincing one's nerves that the World is full of Misery and Heartbreak, Pain, Sickness and oppression — whereby This Chamber of Maiden Thought becomes gradually darken'd and at the same time on all sides of it many doors are set open — but all dark — all leading to dark passages — We see not the ballance of good and evil. We are in a Mist — *We* are now in that state ...
>
> (letter to Reynolds, 3 May 1818)

Though apparently talking in general terms, Keats is talking about his sense of his own development; and he depicts himself as a person on a threshold: the threshold between a 'Chamber of Maiden-Thought', where 'we see nothing but pleasant wonders', and the dark passages beyond, in which we reflect on the miseries of the world. This letter is, in part, an expression of Keats's feeling that he should move on from being a poet of sensuous delights to being a philosopher-poet, able to meditate on the tragic aspects of experience, But the letter depicts Keats as a writer 'in a Mist': a writer poised on a threshold, aware of what lies on both sides, but not yet a writer who has moved across it.

The second instance from his letters does not explicitly mention thresholds, but it is certainly concerned with the value of a threshold-state:

> ... it struck me, what quality went to form a Man of Achievement especially in Literature & which Shakespeare possessed so enormously — I mean *Negative Capability*, that is when man is capable of being in uncertainties, Mysteries, doubts, without any irritable reaching after fact & reason ...
>
> (letter to George and Tom Keats, 21 December 1817)

The term 'Negative Capability' may sound abstract and daunting, but, as Keats defines it, its meaning is clear and straightforward. In this letter he feels that it isn't necessary for him to become a philosopher-poet; indeed, after reflecting on Shakespeare's ability to create numerous different characters and situations, Keats has concluded that his own lack of doctrine or philosophy may be a positive advantage: the threshold-state (when a person is 'capable of being in uncertainties ... without any irritable reaching after fact & reason') is the state in which the poet is free to make forays in many different directions, free to describe sympathetically now a deity and now a sparrow, without being fettered by any doctrine or dogma. What Keats had sometimes regarded as a liability, his apparent philosophical immaturity, could now be regarded as an asset — an impartial freedom. He could make his home on the threshold, instead of feeling obliged to commit himself to any particular region on either side of it. We might even say that Keats's notion of 'Negative Capability' has enabled him to make a doctrine out of a lack of doctrine.

2

In this section, I give examples of the prominence of thresholds, of an obvious kind, in his poems. The first example is one of the most famous of his early sonnets, 'On First Looking into Chapman's Homer':

Much have I travell'd in the realms of gold,
    And many goodly states and kingdoms seen;
    Round many western islands have I been
Which bards in fealty to Apollo hold.
Oft of one wide expanse had I been told
    That deep-brow'd Homer ruled as his demesne;
    Yet did I never breathe its pure serene
Till I heard Chapman speak out loud and bold:
Then felt I like some watcher of the skies
    When a new planet swims into his ken;
Or like stout Cortez when with eagle eyes
    He star'd at the Pacific — and all his men
Look'd at each other with a wild surmise —
    Silent, upon a peak in Darien.

The narrator says that he had long explored the territories of
poetry ('the realms of gold') but had never experienced the
power of Homer's epic writing until he had read Chapman's
Elizabethan translation of Homer, when, suddenly, he felt like
an astronomer discovering a new planet or like the adventurer
Cortez beholding the Pacific. As Cortez stands on the threshold
of the vast ocean, so the narrator stands on the threshold of the
great poetic landscape of Homer — and Chapman's translation
has opened the gateway.

Another threshold, of a very literal kind, is described at the
end of Keats's narrative poem, 'The Eve of St Agnes':

They glide, like phantoms, into the wide hall;
Like phantoms, to the iron porch, they glide;
Where lay the Porter, in uneasy sprawl,
With a huge empty flaggon by his side:
The wakeful bloodhound rose, and shook his hide,
But his sagacious eye an inmate owns:
By one, and one, the bolts full easy slide: —
The chains lie silent on the footworn stones; —
The key turns, and the door upon its hinges groans.

And they are gone: ay, ages long ago
These lovers fled away into the storm.

(ll.361–371)

Porphyro and Madeline are furtively eloping from the castle

owned by Madeline's family, sworn enemies of Porphyro's. It's a perilous escape: if Porphyro is discovered, he will be slain. The lovers, however, are fortunate: the porter lies in a drunken stupor; the bloodhound recognises Madeline, and doesn't bark; so out, across the threshold, they go. But you'll notice that Keats makes it a *double* threshold. As Porphyro and Madeline go outwards, through the great porch, into the storm, so, simultaneously, they seem to step from the imaginative present into the legendary past: 'And they are gone: ay, ages long ago/ These lovers fled away'. We've been moving alongside them, seeing all their actions in close detail, and suddenly they dwindle away into far-off time, into remote and forgotten ages. Instead of a conventionally happy ending to a love-story, we're given a keen sense of the poignancy of time and change.

A further instance of a very conspicuous threshold can be found in Keats's 'The Fall of Hyperion', Canto I. Previously, in 'Hyperion', Keats had attempted to write an epic poem in emulation of Milton's *Paradise Lost*. Milton had begun his epic with an account of the gradual awakening of Satan and the rebel angels after their defeat by God. Keats had begun with a parallel account of the gradual awakening of Saturn and his fellow-Titans after their defeat by Jupiter. Keats's 'Hyperion', however, petered out, incomplete. Later, with 'The Fall of Hyperion', he made a new attempt at the same topic. This new version gives far greater prominence to the poet-narrator himself. In Canto I he imagines himself at the threshold of a vast temple in which a prophetess, Moneta, is tending the shrine. He seeks to climb the steps towards her, but before he reaches them he is stricken almost to death:

> Slow, heavy, deadly was my pace: the cold
> Grew stifling, suffocating, at the heart;
> And when I clasp'd my hands I felt them not.
> One minute before death, my iced foot touch'd
> The lowest stair; and as it touch'd, life seem'd
> To pour in at the toes: I mounted up

(ll.129–134)

After this almost fatal crossing of the threshold, Moneta tells him that though he may regard himself as a poet, he is no better than an idle dreamer; nevertheless, mercifully, she is willing to grant him a vision of the fallen Titans and their saga.

There is, no doubt, a bitterly autobiographical element in that account of the narrator's nearly fatal approach. When he was writing 'The Fall of Hyperion', Keats knew that he was stricken with tuberculosis; already he had suffered bouts of grave illness, feverish, coughing blood from diseased lungs. So that story of the desperate entry to the shrine is, in part, a story of the struggle to resume work on an epic poem after debilitating illness. But there is a further deeply personal element. When the narrator is reproached for being a mere dreamer, Keats is expressing his own misgivings about his poetic ambitions. For part of the time, he was impelled by the ambitious quest to emulate the great poets of the present and past — Wordsworth, Milton, Spenser, all of them authors of works of great scale and scope; yet intermittently Keats experienced doubts not only about his own abilities as a poet, but even about the value of poetry in itself: perhaps, after all, poetry was just fantasy-weaving. He had trained as a surgeon, and knew that there were other, more obviously practical, ways of serving humanity.

Further on in 'The Fall of Hyperion', the poet-narrator hesitates at a further threshold. Moneta has begun to tell the story of the fallen Saturn:

> And she spake on,
> As ye may read who can unwearied pass
> Onward from the Antechamber of this dream,
> Where even at the open doors awhile
> I must delay, and glean my memory
> Of her high phrase: — perhaps no further dare.

(ll.463–468)

In the event, the poet was able to 'dare' only a further 61 lines; and then 'The Fall of Hyperion', like the previous 'Hyperion', petered out, incomplete. So, as it stands, 'The Fall of Hyperion' remains a vast fragment, but a fragment only: it exists as the threshold of an epic, and a threshold on which the poet-narrator and the reader alike remain poised, yet trapped.

One obvious reason for that incompleteness is that, although Keats sometimes had epic ambitions, he did not have the resources or temperament of an epic poet. His strength lay not in the unfolding of a vast philosophical narrative about men and gods, heroes and conquests, but in the ability to record, with thin-skinned sensitivity, intense *moments* of experience. It's in the short poems, particularly the odes like 'Ode to a Nightingale', 'To Autumn' and 'Ode on a Grecian Urn', that this strength is most brilliantly manifest; and, typically, the intense moments recorded concern threshold-states.

3

The 'Ode to a Nightingale' is full of lively oscillations in tone and mood. The narrator is pulled in conflicting directions: now towards death, now towards life; now towards the sensuous pleasures of this world, now towards transcendence of the everyday. In stanza 7, the nightingale, the bird that has sung so rapturously down the ages, seems to offer a promise of immortality:

> Thou wast not born for death, immortal Bird!
> No hungry generations tread thee down;
> The voice I hear this passing night was heard
> In ancient days by emperor and clown

Yet in stanza 8, as commonsense or scepticism reasserts itself, the bird flies away, dwindling from timelessness to the temporal:

> Adieu! adieu! thy plaintive anthem fades
> Past the near meadows, over the still stream,
>   Up the hill-side; and now 'tis buried deep
>   In the next valley-glades:
> Was it a vision, or a waking dream?
> Fled is that music: — Do I wake or sleep?

'Do I wake or sleep?' In other words, 'Have I awakened into common sense, or have I fallen into the slumber which is mere everyday reality? Did the nightingale offer me a true vision of immortality and transcendence, or was I merely day-dreaming?' The power of the poem lies in the sensuous vigour with which all these alternatives are presented, so that the reader, too, enacts a threshold-experience: a state of vivid ambiguity.

'To Autumn' seems much less ambiguous: a rich evocation

of the diverse pleasures of that season. It's still unconventional. Most poetic treatments of autumn tend to be melancholy, depicting it as the sad decline of the year towards winter; but although the last stanza of Keats's ode points hints at that decline ('The red-breast whistles from a garden-croft;/ And gathering swallows twitter in the skies'), the first two stanzas emphasise the full abundance that we often associate with late summer: apples, honey, harvest. By reminding us of warm bountiful days as well as the cooler misty times to come, the poem makes autumn seem much more of a threshold-state, the location of multiple changes and transitions, than is customarily the case. Hence, largely, the pleasures of 'To Autumn', which is no dirge for a dying year but a celebration of a diversity of sensuous enjoyments.

As for 'Ode on a Grecian Urn', it's a poem all about a threshold-object: for the urn itself, as depicted by Keats, is itself the threshold of the temporal and the timeless, the mortal and the immortal. Brilliantly this ode confuses our sense of the contrast between the familiar world of the living and the strange other-world of ancient but enduring art. We are offered paradox upon paradox. The urn offers both a 'Cold Pastoral' and images of love 'for ever warm and still to be enjoy'd'; the 'still' urn depicts 'mad pursuit' and 'wild ecstasy'; and this 'foster-child of silence' plays 'ditties of no tone'; 'Heard melodies are sweet, but those unheard/ Are sweeter'. No wonder that it can 'tease us out of thought/ As doth eternity'. And typically, when the urn finally offers us a maxim from its store:

Beauty is truth, truth beauty . . .

(l.49)

it offers us a maxim which is true to its enigmatic, paradox-loving character. Just like the notion of eternity, the claim 'Beauty is truth, truth beauty' can 'tease us out of thought': for, like the word 'eternity', that claim makes an obvious, immediate kind of sense; but just as the imagination finds it impossible to grasp clearly and fully the extent of eternity, so the mind struggles and flinches when called on to explain adequately the meaning of 'Beauty is truth'. It's a threshold-statement: it stands precisely on the threshold between the obvious and the inscrutable.

AFTERTHOUGHTS

1

Explain the ways in which Watts is using the term 'thresholds' in this essay.

2

Do *you* find the meaning of 'Negative Capability' to be 'clear and straightforward' (page 11)? What do you take it to mean?

3

How relevant do you find it to an understanding of 'The Fall of Hyperion' to be aware of its 'bitterly autobiographical element' (page 14)?

4

What do you understand by the closing sentence of this essay?

Peter Cairns

Peter Cairns is Head of English and Drama at Dean Close School, Cheltenham and an experienced A- level examiner. He has edited several school texts for Longman.

ESSAY

The sense of transience in the poems of 1819

Transience, the impermanence of things, is the theme of the four seriously philosophical poems of John Keats. These are the Odes: to a Nightingale, on a Grecian Urn, on Melancholy, and the dream-poem 'The Fall of Hyperion'. These poems present and discuss the threat of time, and develop towards the final and essential Keatsian attitude of 'wakeful anguish' described in the 'Ode on Melancholy', that divine insight which the dreaming poet is granted in 'The Fall of Hyperion':

> A power within me of enormous ken
> To see as God sees. . .

> (ll.303–304)

However, the *sense* of transience pervades all the poems of 1819. The list is astonishingly varied; it contains tragedy and epic, odes and sonnets, fairy tales and lyrical ballads. The feel of things fading is in all of them; not just in pictures of a dying brother, 'pale, and spectre thin' ('Ode to a Nightingale'), or the doomed Saturn ('Hyperion') or the haggard knight-at-arms ('La Belle Dame sans Merci'); but also associated with those very images which celebrate the rich intensity of life and beauty most excitedly.

Each of these poems expresses in varying degrees and in many different ways the greater intensity of experience and increased value of life when in close contact with death. 'Death is Life's high meed', wrote Keats in the sonnet 'Why did I laugh tonight?': awareness of it makes life more precious, love more intense, beauty more poignant. The ability to convey this is the rarest and most heroic attribute of a poet. In December 1817, it seemed inexpressible:

> The feel of not to feel it,
> When there is none to heal it,
> Nor numbed sense to steal it,
>   Was never said in rhyme.
>   ('Stanzas: In a drear-nighted December . . .', stanza III)

Nevertheless, this sense of transience is described in the most important of the odes. Keats, accepting the suggestion of the early-seventeenth-century writer Robert Burton, calls the attitude 'Melancholy'.

The 'Ode on Melancholy' is in some ways unsatisfactory. The missing first stanza causes a clumsy start; the clichés of melancholy behaviour in classical or neo-classical times mean little to us now; and we may be distracted from the dewy beauties of spring so beautifully caught at the beginning of stanza 2 by the thought of the staring poet receiving a well-deserved smack in the mouth from the angry mistress:

> Or if thy mistress some rich anger shows,
> Emprison her soft hand, and let her rave,
> And feed deep, deep upon her peerless eyes.

However, the third stanza is perfect. It explains the 'truth' about 'Beauty' more clearly than the famous but vague lines in the 'Ode on a Grecian Urn', while conveying the sense of beauty enjoyed and lost in a single moment as poignantly as anywhere in poetry:

> She dwells with Beauty — Beauty that must die;
>   And Joy whose hand is ever at his lips
> Bidding adieu; and aching Pleasure nigh,
>   Turning to poison while the bee-mouth sips:
> Ay, in the very temple of Delight

Veil'd Melancholy has her sovran shrine,
　　Though seen of none save him whose strenuous tongue
Can burst Joy's grape against his palate fine:
　　His soul shall taste the sadness of her might,
　　And be among her cloudy trophies hung.

Here are three or four images of intense life. The first is a dramatically visual scene of lovers parting, the sweet sorrow of separation; next, a complex fusion of pictures: perhaps a beautiful face expressing some ambiguous ecstasy, changing to the bee in a garden of summer flowers; lastly an extraordinary communication of the sensation of taste: the explosion of cool flavour suggested by the reader's muscular involvement in the sound of the words 'whose strenuous tongue/ Can burst Joy's grape against his palate fine'. But these images flash at us only momentarily in the dark temple of 'veil'd Melancholy' and are lost in the clouds of sadness, among those trophies which seem like tombs.

The sense of transience is often conveyed in this way: by the structural device of framing which creates a feeling of perspective. Vivid dream-images of love and beauty are placed behind a foreground or framework of history or reality which makes for a sense of distance and loss. Keats tells stories about the unattainable past. Nearly every poem presents pictures of remote lost worlds of ancient Greece or the Middle Ages. The Hyperion story to which Keats devoted so much precious time focuses on the end of an age of time: on the moment of change from one divine dynasty to another, from Titan to Olympian, from Hyperion to Apollo.

The introductions and endings to the narrative poems distance us from the settings with insistent medieval detail and archaic language: Sabbath bells, 'fireside orat'ries' and an 'arched porch' for example in 'The Eve of St Mark', a knight-at-arms, kings and princes in 'La Belle Dame sans Merci', whose very name is that of a medieval French poem.

Of 'The Eve of St Mark' and the Hyperion poems we have only the introductions, as they were unfinished. However in two finished poems of the narrative type, the effectiveness of structure in conveying the sense of transience can be clearly recognised.

The story in 'The Eve of St Agnes' is like *Romeo and Juliet* with a happy ending. Commentators have noted how untypical that ending is of Keats's poetry. Nevertheless the atmosphere of the poem is completely characteristic because of the sense we have throughout of the fragility of love, happiness and beauty. The dazzling psychedelic images of windows, feasts and Madeline are surrounded by clouds of darkness, cold, winter, old age and death. The introductory stanzas convey every cold sensation of the winter night:

> The sculptur'd dead, on each side, seem to freeze,
> Emprison'd in black, purgatorial rails:
> Knights, ladies, praying in dumb orat'ries,
> He passeth by; and his weak spirit fails
> To think how they may ache in icy hoods and mails.
>
> (ll.14–18)

In the third stanza the sudden dramatic impact of 'Music's golden tongue' shows how pervasively the world of darkness and death has been established.

Throughout the poem images of beauty are introduced or framed by alien, contrasting impressions of darkness and danger. Madeline in stanza VIII is seen:

> 'Mid looks of love, defiance, hate and scorn,
> Hoodwink'd with faery fancy . . .
>
> (ll.69–70)

Porphyro enters the castle whose

> . . . chambers held barbarian hordes,
> Hyena foemen, and hot-blooded lords,
> Whose very dogs would execrations howl
> Against his lineage . . .
>
> (ll.85–88)

The lovers are helped by the aged crone, Angela; but her presence and that of the old Beadsman seems to haunt their future. The sudden burst of vivid colour in stanzas XXIV and XXV where the moon shines through the stained-glass window on Madeline at her prayers is approached through three stanzas where there is no colour but spectral grey and darkness. The effect is of sudden dramatic contrast. Compare the colour associations of these words: 'dusky', 'agues', 'pallid', 'faltering', 'old', 'spirit', 'silver-taper', ring-dove', and 'spirit' again, with 'garlanded', 'fruits', 'flowers', 'bunches of knot grass', 'diamonded', 'stains', 'splendid dyes', 'tiger', 'tiger-moth's deep damask'd wings', 'heraldries', 'emblazonings', 'blush'd', 'blood', 'queens and kings'.

The elements of the plot are the same as those in most of the late poems. There is a lady, a dream, feasting, courtship and a cold awakening. Unlike the knight-at-arms, the poet in the 'Ode to a Nightingale' or Lycius in 'Lamia', Porphyro and Madeline are not permanently forlorn at the intrusion of reality. Initially:

> There was a painful change, that nigh expell'd
> The blisses of her dream so pure and deep
> At which poor Madeline began to weep
>
> (ll.300–302)

Then the dream of love becomes, it would seem, the act of love:

> Into her dream he melted, as the rose
> Blendeth its odour with the violet
>
> (ll.320–321)

But the ecstasy lasts no more than a few lines: the winter is still there:

> Solution sweet: meantime the frost-wind blows
> Like Love's alarum pattering the sharp sleet
> Against the window panes; St Agnes' moon hath set.
>
> (ll.322–324)

At the end the lovers seem to be winners. Past a series of detailed and atmospheric images — the torches, tapestries and wind-blown carpets; the drunken porter reminding us perhaps of the horrors of Macbeth's castle; the groaning hinges of the door — they flee into the storm. Nevertheless the enduring impression at the end of the poem is of the winter which must surely have caught them in the end. The last stanza, like a receding camera, takes us farther and farther away from the happiness of the lovers through a collage of images of death:

> And they are gone: ay, ages long ago
> These lovers fled away into the storm.
> That night the Baron dreamt of many a woe,
> And all his warrior-guests, with shade and form
> Of witch, and demon, and large coffin-worm,
> Were long be-nightmar'd. Angela the old
> Died palsy-twitch'd, with meagre face deform;
> The Beadsman, after thousand aves told,
> For aye unsought for slept among his ashes cold.

(ll.370–378)

The skeletal faces, deformed by nightmare, disease and death, take us back to the Beadsman, with whose life of suffering the poem started.

The other arguably 'perfect' poem, shorter and simpler, demonstrates this relationship between structural features and the sense of transience even more clearly. In 'La Belle Dame sans Merci' the knight has enjoyed ideal love, beauty, music, feasting and rest; but such happiness is at best momentary, probably illusory, and its only effect has been to leave his life empty, lonely and meaningless, as the countryside grows colder, and winter approaches.

The poem begins and ends with the same picture, the same words. The impressions are of sickness, solitude and the death of summer in a remote medieval world cursed by evil spells:

> O what can ail thee, knight-at-arms,
>   Alone and palely loitering?
> The sedge has wither'd from the lake,
>   And no birds sing.

As in 'The Eve of St Agnes' the threat of time is felt at the beginning and the end. However, the pictures contained in the frame of the shorter poem are less vivid. Wild eyes, garlands, bracelets, fragrant girdles, wild honey and glistening dewdrops contrast effectively with the bleak scene; but their impact is brief, subdued by the sad cadence of this distinctive ballad form:

> And I awoke and found me here,
>   On the cold hill's side.

(ll.43–44)

The control of cadence, the dying fall of stanza and poem, is an essential feature in Keats's finest works, and is perhaps the chief instrument in conveying the sense of transience.

Keats delighted in the more demanding stanza forms and exploited the dramatic and lyrical possibilities of each with the skill of a great composer. He was concerned always with the way the form would affect the sound, in particular the sound of the end of a verse or poem. In three poems he employed looser patterns. In the two Hyperion poems he made use of Miltonic blank verse and it is perhaps significant that this seems only to have led the poet in a circle, before it was abandoned as unsatisfactory. The couplets of 'Lamia', borrrowed from Dryden's versions of Chaucer, are chiefly remarkable for the use of variants, such as the triplet, and the hexameter, a twelve-syllable line which makes for a heavy cadence, as at the end of the poem:

> On the high couch he lay! — his friends came round —
> Supported him — no pulse, or breath they found,
> And, in its marriage robe, the heavy body wound.

It would seem that Keats preferred more elaborate and varied patterns, especially stanza forms with distinctive cadences or endings. The comparison of a less successful narrative poem with the perfectly rounded 'Eve of St Agnes' demonstrates this. The stanza form of 'Isabella' (written in March 1818) is the 'ottava rima', an eight-line stanza of pentameters rhyming *ababab cc*. The form is demanding enough, insisting as it does on only three rhymes, and the final couplet creates a strong cadence; but although this striking pattern is often vigorous and declamatory, its use is not essentially related to the character or atmosphere of the story. Even in stanza XIV, one of the more successful verses where Keats's descriptive skills are clearly evident, the couplet adds little to the overall effect:

> With her two brothers this fair lady dwelt,
>   Enriched from ancestral merchandize,
> And for them many a weary hand did swelt
>   In torched mines and noisy factories,
> And many once proud-quiver'd loins did melt

In blood from stinging whip; — with hollow eyes
Many all day in dazzling river stood,
To take the rich-ored driftings of the flood.

The form used in 'The Eve of St Agnes' is the Spenserian stanza of nine lines: two regular pentameter quatrains rounded off with a hexameter. The rhyme scheme is *ababbcbcc*. The form was invented by the Elizabethan poet Edmund Spenser for his great poem *The Faerie Queene*. The reading of Spenser's poetry had first inspired Keats to write poetry five years previously, and this stanza form certainly plays an important part in the success of this poem.

The distinctive sound of the poem derives of course from the cadence which again and again reinforces the overall atmosphere. Each stanza ends with a longer line which is also part of a couplet. The effect is firstly of completeness, self-containment: the poem has been described as a series of self-contained pictures. The other effect is of heaviness, sometimes weariness as in the stanzas on the Beadsman:

Another way he went, and soon among
Rough ashes sat he for his soul's reprieve
And all night kept awake, for sinners' sake to grieve.

(ll.25–27)

Again and again the sound of that long last line conveys the sadness of a dying fall, the feel of transience, never more effectively than at the end:

The Beadsman, after thousand aves told,
For aye unsought for slept among his ashes cold.

Contrastingly, in 'La Belle Dame sans Merci', the sad or menacing rhythms are largely the effect of a shorter last line. The simple language and the apparent simplicity of the ballad form help to establish the medieval setting and to suggest the ingenuous recounting of a dream-like experience, as in Coleridge's ballad *The Rime of the Ancient Mariner*. However, the feel of this poem is very different. This is not only because of the stillness of the scene: it is due to the rhythmic effect of the last line, often only four syllables long, but usually containing three heavy stresses. The effect is to slow the rhythm to a pause each time, but also of words echoing in a silence. Also the stressed words are those which convey most emotively the menacing approach of winter or death, particularly at the beginning and end of the poem:

> And no birds sing.   (stanza I)
> And the harvest's done.   (stanza II)
> Fast withereth too.   (stanza III)

Two lines are used twice, with haunting effect in the last two stanzas:

> On the cold hill's side.   (stanza XI)
> And no birds sing.   (stanza XII)

In his lyrical ballad then, Keats employs most effectively the two structural devices of framing and cadence to convey the doomed quality of human happiness. Robert Gittings who in his book *The Living Year* (London, 1954) writes interestingly about the background to these poems suggests:

> The story of 'La Belle Dame ' is, among all its other elements, the story of Keats's dead brother and the cruel deception that first his friends, and then life itself, had played upon him — the delivery of his youth to disappointment and death. It gains for us its poignancy ... from a circumstance unseen to Keats — that within two years he himself was to go the way of his brother and to join him among the death-pale crowd.

Before Keats wrote his odes in the spring and summer of 1819, he wrote several sonnets. A distinctive feature of the sonnet form, apart from the strict discipline it imposes, is the choice of cadence it offers in the last six lines, the sestet. Keats wrote both Shakespearian sonnets, in which the sestet is a third quatrain and a couplet, and Petrarchan sonnets, in which the sestet has various permutations of rhyme, often *efg efg*. It is significant that the form he chose for his odes is a reduced Petrarchan sonnet: the last ten of the fourteen lines, as it were. Again, it was the cadence which interested him.

The 'Ode to a Nightingale', the first of the last four odes, is the saddest. It contains vivid sensuous delights, but they are illusions experienced only through drugs and dreams. The first section ends with another reminder of his brother Tom Keats's death and a harrowing presentation of transience and mortality, facts of life which the nightingale has never known:

> The weariness, the fever, and the fret
>> Here, where men sit and hear each other groan;
> Where palsy shakes a few, sad, last gray hairs,
>> Where youth grows pale and spectre-thin, and dies

$$(\text{ll.}23\text{--}26)$$

The echoing word 'forlorn' introduces the last stanza and a feeling of desolation and bewilderment. Again the cadence creates a sense of distance and loss:

> Adieu! adieu! thy plaintive anthem fades
>> Past the near meadows, over the still stream,
>>> Up the hill-side; and now 'tis buried deep
>>>> In the next valley-glades:
> Was it a vision, or a waking dream?
>> Fled is that music: — Do I wake or sleep?

The form is like the sestet of a sonnet: the long, drawn-out rhyme pattern seems to contribute to the distancing effect. This is the only ode with a short line, and its use is dramatic and poignant. In most stanzas it contains key emotive words and disturbs the flow of the music, but it is in stanza 3 that the pause is most expressive:

> Where but to think is to be full of sorrow
>> And leaden-eyed despairs

In 'Ode on a Grecian Urn' and 'Ode on Melancholy' the power of time is still felt, but the mood is not one of defeat. The sense of loss is balanced by the consolations of art and philosophy, or at least an attitude of mind. In these poems the stanza form, still ten lines of a Petrarchan sonnet, has an appropriately dignified regularity.

In 'To Autumn', the meaning of the 'Ode on Melancholy' is marvellously demonstrated, not least through the poet's mastery of form and cadence. The poem communicates an experience of beauty that is simultaneous with a serene acceptance of its transience. There is a moment of absolute ripeness: the culmination of the past balanced by a sense of future loss. The feeling of fellowship or communion in nature's triumphal feast will, we know, die away when the swallows leave the red-breast behind to face the winter. Commentators have noted the sequence of sense impressions through the three stanzas: of touch and taste in verse 1, of sight in verse 2, and of sound in the last verse. In verse 3, the sense of transience is expressed poignantly but unobtrusively by the rhythms, which are controlled by stanza form, rhyme pattern, and cadence.

The stanza this time has eleven lines. The second quatrain and the sestet of a Petrarchan sonnet are extended by one line: seven of the eleven lines of the stanza seem to make up its ending:

> Then in a wailful choir the small gnats mourn
>   Among the river sallows, borne aloft
>   Or sinking as the light wind lives or dies;
> And full-grown lambs loud bleat from hilly bourn;
>   Hedge-crickets sing; and now with treble soft
> The red-breast whistles from a garden-croft;
>   And gathering swallows twitter in the skies.

The rhyme scheme is *cdecdde*. The rhyming words have drawn-out vowel sounds, the sad dying fall of 'mourn' and 'dies'; but the extra rhyme from 'soft' to 'croft' in the couplet, placed influentially near the end, has a comforting gentleness. Although the image in the last line is ominously sad, there is an immediacy in the rhythms, in which the sound echoes the sense, which makes the final impression not of sadness, but just of being there, watching and listening. We are, as it were, pressing Joy's grape against the palate.

AFTERTHOUGHTS

1

Do you agree with Cairns's claim that the third stanza of the 'Ode on Melancholy' 'explains the "truth" about "beauty" more clearly than the famous but vague lines in the "Ode on a Grecian Urn"' (page 19)?

2

What do you understand by 'the structural device of framing' (page 20)?

3

How helpful do you find it to consider Keats's narrative technique in terms of the cinema (see, for example, the reference to a 'receding camera' on page 22)?

4

What do you understand by the terms 'cadence', 'dying fall' and 'ballad form' (pages 23–24)?

Brean Hammond

Brean Hammond is Lecturer in English Literature at the University of Liverpool, and has written numerous critical studies.

ESSAY

John Keats: two types of sexuality

In this essay, I intend to concentrate on three of Keats's major poems, 'The Eve of St Agnes', the 'Ode on a Grecian Urn' and the ode 'To Autumn'. First, though, I will spend some time discussing a truly terrifying poem by one of the 'first generation' romantic poets, Samuel Coleridge. 'Christabel' is an unfinished narrative poem set in the grounds and interior of a medieval baronial castle. It is so influential on 'The Eve of St Agnes' that it could be described as the pre-text for the later poem. Keats recasts narrative elements of the earlier poem to tell his own story. Reading both poems in conjunction will make us sensitive to the way romantic narrative poems take on levels of meaning beyond or below the story. Details of the stories they tell assume a symbolic power, which reaches, in works like the *The Rime of the Ancient Mariner*, *Frankenstein* and *Prometheus Unbound*, into areas of psychological uncertainty — loneliness, speechlessness, sexual trauma.

In the first part of 'Christabel', the lady leaves the security of her father's Hall at midnight to go out into the forest because she has been troubled by dreams about 'her own betrothed knight'. Praying beneath an oak tree, Christabel hears a low moaning sound. The moaner turns out to be a beautiful, richly dressed lady called Geraldine, who explains that she was abducted by five unknown men and abandoned in this spot. Christabel offers Geraldine the sanctuary of her father's Hall, but as she takes Geraldine inside, there are many suspicious signs that this 'taking in' is dangerous. Nature herself and even the very architecture of the Hall seem to oppose this ingress. Geraldine has to be carried across the threshold by Christabel, like the travesty of a bride. She 'cannot speak for weariness' when Christabel offers praise to the Virgin. Possibly she has little affinity with virgins? The watchdog, a 'mastiff bitch', fails to awaken when they pass, yet makes an 'angry moan'. Passing the dying embers of the fire, 'there came/ A tongue of light, a fit of flame;/ And Christabel saw the lady's eye,/ And nothing else saw she thereby' except the boss of her father's shield, a reminder, perhaps, of the authority they are abusing. Searching for her lover, Christabel finds instead the lady Geraldine, whose story cannot be verified. We feel that the worst thing Christabel can do is to take her inside. Having gained Christabel's bedroom, Geraldine successfully struggles with what appears to be the protective spirit of the girl's dead mother; and having ordered Christabel to undress and go to bed she shows Christabel the hideous truth about her own naked body, a truth that, in the best horror-story tradition, is not revealed to the reader. She then pronounces a curse on Christabel. Christabel will possess the knowledge of the appalling truth about her, but will not be able to speak that knowledge to others. She will be a secret sharer in an evil that cannot be divulged.

Throughout, the reader is sensitive to a certain pressure behind the story of Geraldine's admittance. The details, the various signs that Christabel ignores, are enacting a drama. It is a drama of the violation of security that is easily translatable into the terms of a sexual allegory. Geraldine's femininity, her sexual similarity to Christabel, is not a protection but, oddly, is felt as very much more threatening than an illicit male presence would be. As in other romantic works, a journey is as much an inner journey, a penetration of the dark places of the mind and body, as it is a geographical exploration. Keats's 'The Eve of St Agnes' utilises some of the elements of the 'Christabel' story — a story, also, of penetration, of the exploitation and violation of innocence.

It is St Agnes's Eve, a night on which, according to popular superstition, virgins might receive visits from their lovers in dreams, provided they use the correct observances. (Christabel is actually having such dreams, but involuntarily.) Madeline, the heroine of the poem, is discovered in the Great Hall of her father's castle, brooding on these old wives' tales, lonely in the midst of dancing and revelry. She intends to withdraw into her chamber and put the story to the test. 'Meantime', as the poet puts it, the object of Madeline's dreams, young Porphyro, is making his way bodily to her. As with Geraldine, Porphyro's gaining access seems a kind of violation, more obviously a penetration of hostile space, because there is a feud going on between his family and hers (as there is in 'Christabel' between her father and the father that Geraldine claims as hers, Sir Roland de Vaux of Tryermaine). In 'Christabel', there is something menacing, not accidental, about the meeting of the girl and the woman behind the oak tree. What kind of coincidence is this meeting, the reader asks? Is it coincidence, or were the troublesome dreams in some way visited upon Christabel, a means of summoning her? In Keats's poem, the same question arises. What kind of convergence is it that brings Madeline and Porphyro together on this night of all nights? Is this coincidence, or does he intend to take advantage of the girl's naïveté and substitute his reality for her dreaming vision?

Porphyro's motive is never spelled out in the poem beyond stanza IX. In a famous letter to his brothers written on 21 December 1817, Keats encapsulated the nature of poetic genius in the phrase 'Negative Capability':

> . . . at once it struck me, what quality went to form a Man of Achievement especially in Literature & which Shakespeare possessed so enormously — I mean *Negative Capability*, that is when a man is capable of being in uncertainties, Mysteries, doubts, without any irritable reaching after fact & reason.

In the uncertainties, mysteries and doubts surrounding the unstated motives of the lovers, the poem's appeal lies. Interesting that Keats should mention Shakespeare in this connection, because 'The Eve of St Agnes' is very Shakespearean in design. Porphyro, prevented from gaining access to Madeline by the family blood-feud, is led to her by the panderism of Angela, who plays a similar role to the nurse in *Romeo and Juliet*. The simile Keats uses to express the conception of Porphyro's plan to invade the sanctity of Madeline's bedroom is that of the rose, and it is the first of a chain of rose images that have a precise function:

> Sudden a thought came like a full-blown rose,
> Flushing his brow, and in his pained heart
> Made purple riot . . .

(ll.136–138)

This 'thought' is given by the image an unnatural maturity, and the physical symptoms it produces are not unambiguously pleasant, not altogether separable from guilt and decadence. If you know it, you might be reminded of William Blake's symbolic poem 'The Sick Rose' that is often read as an allegory of furtive and diseased sexual union:

> O rose, thou art sick!
> The invisible worm
> That flies in the night,
> In the howling storm,
>
> Has found out thy bed
> Of crimson joy,
> And his dark secret love
> Does thy life destroy.

Although Porphyro protests, in stanza XVII, that he doesn't intend to harm his loved one — or even to touch her — the unfolding of the plan in stanza XIX is ambivalent:

> Which was, to lead him, in close secrecy,
> Even to Madeline's chamber, and there hide
> Him in a closet, of such privacy
> That he might see her beauty unespied,
> And win perhaps that night a peerless bride

(ll.163–167)

Are Porphyro's desires entirely voyeuristic, or do they include the wish for actual sexual possession? Angela, at least, is pretty certain what he's after and, with her limited, respectable point of view, her concern is only that he should do the decent thing:

'Ah! thou must needs the lady wed,/ Or may I never leave my grave among the dead' (ll.179–180). When we see Madeline in her entranced, somnambulistic state in stanza XXIII, what strikes us perhaps is the continuing presentiment of threat and danger. She is under the same spell of silence as was Christabel, a state that Keats specifies as one of inexpressive art or unexpressable beauty:

> No uttered syllable, or, woe betide!
> But to her heart, her heart was voluble,
> Paining with eloquence her balmy side;
> As though a tongueless nightingale should swell
> Her throat in vain, and die, heart-stifled, in her dell.
>
> (ll.203–207)

Stanza XXV introduces a new element in the presentation of Madeline. She is created as an art-object by the modulations of moonlight through the filters of different-coloured glass:

> Full on this casement shone the wintry moon,
> And threw warm gules on Madeline's fair breast,
> As down she knelt for heaven's grace and boon;
> Rose-bloom fell on her hands, together pressed,
> And on her silver cross soft amethyst,
> And on her hair a glory, like a saint.
>
> (ll.217–222)

The heraldic colours create Madeline as a saint in a religious icon, so that 'She seem'd a splendid angel, newly drest/ Save wings, for heaven'. This works as a kind of protection, because Porphyro is forced to confront the purity, the chastity, the inviolability, of art. Is there, though, something disturbing about the 'rose-bloom' on her hands, preserving the continuity of her lover's unclean thoughts — the 'full-blown rose'? A little later, when Madeline is naked but protected by the innocence of sleep, the image used to render her innocence is one of the rose returning to the bud (1.243), an image of sexual immaturity. By stanza XXVIII, where the diction is Miltonic, alluding to Satan's watching Eve in *Paradise Lost* 9.494ff, the reader is, I believe, beginning to entertain severe doubts about Porphyro's enterprise.

To his friend Benjamin Bailey on 22 November 1817, Keats

had written that 'The Imagination may be compared to Adam's dream — he awoke and found it truth'. The climactic stanzas of the poem dramatise just such an awakening. Madeline is to wake, and when she does, it will be impossible for her to know whether she is dreaming or awake, because the object of her waking perception is exactly the same as that of her dream vision: the bending figure of her lover. Yet it is at once apparent that to Madeline, the reality is no adequate substitute for the dream. The language of stanzas XXXIV and XXXV is that of disillusion, of disappointment, of anticlimax:

> There was a painful change, that nigh expell'd
> The blisses of her dream so pure and deep
> At which fair Madeline began to weep,
> And moan forth witless words with many a sigh;
> While still her gaze on Porphyro would keep;
> Who knelt, with joined hands and piteous eye,
> Fearing to move or speak, she look'd so dreamingly.

> 'Ah, Porphyro!', said she, 'but even now
> 'Thy voice was at sweet tremble in mine ear,
> 'Made tuneable with every sweetest vow;
> 'And those, sad eyes were spiritual and clear;
> 'How chang'd thou art! how pallid, chill, and drear!
> 'Give me that voice again, my Porphyro,
> 'Those looks immortal, those complainings dear!

(ll.300–313)

The famous line from the 'Ode on a Grecian Urn' (to which we will return) comes to mind: 'Heard melodies are sweet, but those unheard/ Are sweeter'. Madeline is now hearing the melody. Under the circumstances, it is ironic that these 'voluptuous accents', with their unflattering words, are to Porphyro the aphrodisiac that turns mere contemplation into possession. Again, the image of the rose is the image of consummation; but this time, it is also an image of adulteration, an almost unnatural horticultural experiment:

> Into her dream he melted, as the rose
> Blendeth its odour with the violet

(ll.320–321)

Immediately, consummation brings on a post-coital phase, depicted in images of frost, sharp sleet against the window panes and 'iced gusts'. 'St Agnes' moon has set' comes to seem like a bitter epitaph on Madeline's maidenly hopes. Stanza XXXVII brings, so to speak, the first lovers' tiff — and the final stanzas of the poem are furtive, as the lovers guiltily abscond. The drama of Geraldine's intrusion is played out in reverse in the elopement of Madeline and Porphyro. Coleridge's 'mastiff bitch' finds an ironic counterpart in Keats's 'wakeful bloodhound' that recognises its mistress and does not give the alarm. Inanimate objects — the arras and the carpet — and drunken animate ones alike fail to prevent the elopement as in 'Christabel' they failed to prevent the violation. And the Baron is left to his nightmares.

My reading of 'The Eve of St Agnes' figures the desire for sexual possession as a serpent in the garden of innocence. Porphyro wants to enter Madeline's secret places: first her chamber, then the secret places of her imagination as he literally inserts himself into her dreams, and finally her most secret place of all — her body. His desires, at first voyeuristic, finally embrace a wish for actual physical possession. There are two different models for sexuality here which, in the 'Ode on a Grecian Urn', become the basis for two different possibilities for art. The conflicting claims of erotic anticipation and erotic satisfaction, of contemplation against possession, are made in 'The Eve of St Agnes' through Madeline's roles as art-object and sex-object. As the German philosopher Kant had argued in his *Critique of Judgement*, aesthetic attention is a 'disinterested' kind of attention. To attend to a painting, say, is to regard it with a kind of interest that has no practical purpose, no desire for ownership. Keats put the point amusingly to John Hamilton Reynolds:

> We hate poetry that has a palpable design upon us — and, if we do not agree, seems to put its hand in its breeches pocket. Poetry should be great & unobtrusive, a thing which enters into one's soul, and does not startle it or amaze it with itself, but with its subject. — How beautiful are the retired flowers! How would they lose their beauty were they to throng into the highway crying out, 'Admire me, I am a violet! dote upon me I am a primrose!'
>
> (letter, 3 February 1818)

I find 'The Eve of St Agnes' unambiguous about preferring the erotics of contemplation to the erotics of possession and I think that the disinterested view of art it implies squares well with the quotation given above.

The 'Ode on a Grecian Urn' is a not-so-straightforward consideration of the same area. The urn is at first presented as a 'Sylvan historian', a story-teller of the woods; and the poet compares its pictorial medium favourably to his own verbal one. Yet if the urn does tell a story, it is one that the reader is unable to understand. Stanza 1 disperses into questions that are never answered in the poem. If, as is sometimes said, art has to do with communication, then this art-object must strike us as unsatisfactory, representing a form of experience that is mysterious and unintelligible. The paradoxical statement that opens the second stanza is, we understand, a metaphorical declaration of the view that the world of the imagination is superior to the world of sensuality — what Madeline learns in the 'Eve of St Agnes'. As such, it is an important encapsulation of one powerful strand in romantic aesthetics. True sensuality is to be found in anticipation rather than in consummation. Timelessness of the arrested moment is offered as complete compensation for absence of satisfaction. This insight is developed in the third stanza. With its repetitions of 'happy' and 'for ever', the diction imitates the quality of pleasure depicted on the urn. If the artistic decoration of the urn excludes satisfaction, it also excludes all possibility of death and decay, of mutability and change. This is the definitive difference between *art*, as represented on the urn, and *life*. But at this point the reader may begin to experience disquiet. Might we not suspect that this eternal erotic teasing is sterile, belonging to the auto-erotic realm of the sexual voyeur? To at least one modern poet, Wallace Stevens, this has seemed to be the case. His 'Sunday Morning' triumphantly affirms that 'Death is the mother of beauty', impatiently dismissing the paradisal vision that depends on stasis and timelessness:

> Is there no change of death in paradise?
> Does ripe fruit never fall? Or do the boughs
> Hang always heavy in that perfect sky?

In my reading of 'Grecian Urn', Keats himself begins to feel something of this sterility, because in stanza 4, he returns to the business of interrogating the urn, only to find that another quality it possesses 'for evermore' is that of the inexplicable. The customs and religious observances of the urn people are utterly foreign to later spectators. Somehow, the image of the heifer doomed to repeat endlessly its fate of being led to the sacrificial altar is much less pleasing than that of the everlasting lovers of stanza 2 and the everlasting spring of stanza 3. The heifer's 'lowing at the skies' can seem to be a protest at the unintelligible injustice of the 'mysterious priest' and the town, 'emptied', 'silent', 'desolate' and quite literally soulless, seems a far cry from the earlier celebration. By stanza 5, the 'Sylvan historian' of the opening has become a 'Cold Pastoral'. Both the urn as art-object and the *coitus interruptus* sensuality that it depicts have failed to persuade us altogether of their appeal and Keats can only end the poem by doing violence to its own integrity. Much debate has centred on the ending of the poem, both on the precise interpretation to be given of the lines, and on the question whether it is a didactic ending to a poem that ought to refuse to offer such closure. Although the 'message' is not unambiguous (so that those who argue the poem to be firmly closed are perhaps exaggerating) it is clearly a message of sorts, not impossible to paraphrase — the way of poetic apprehension is superior to the philosophical or religious quest for certainty. To this extent, I do find that the poet has forced the poem to do what the urn has conspicuously refused to do. Is it too fanciful to think of the poet's questioning of the urn as, in the end, an attempt to ravish the 'bride of quietness'?

My point, then, about the ode would be that the uncertainty of the poem suggests a growing impatience with the erotics of contemplation. If there is an escape from the dilemma of contemplation that breeds frustration and possession that is a rape, it takes the form, in Keats, of a timeless moment, an instant lifted out of the flux of time and held in suspension, or perhaps a moment of fusion that is destroyed in the instant of its happening. To me the most memorable images in Keats are those of frozen movement, movement arrested and held in tableau or rigidified into an 'attitude'. When, in an early sonnet, Keats evokes his excited discovery of Chapman's translation of Homer, he renders the experience in a sculpture of astonishment:

> Then felt I like some watcher of the skies
>   When a new planet swims into his ken;
> Or like stout Cortez when with eagle eyes
>   He star'd at the Pacific — and all his men
> Look'd at each other with a wild surmise —
>   Silent, upon a peak in Darien.
>
>   (ll.9–14)

Or in 'Hyperion', where Thea and Saturn are figured 'postured motionless,/ Like natural sculpture in cathedral cavern;/ The frozen God still couchant on the earth,/ And the sad Goddess weeping at his feet' (ll.85–88). In the ode 'To Autumn', there is, I think, a final move towards an erotics of possession that was seen as entirely destructive in 'The Eve of St Agnes'. And the image of arrested movement is in the later ode employed to celebrate a sensuality based on fertility, fulfilment and procreation.

A common critical reaction to the ode 'To Autumn' is to praise what seems to be its perfection. Walter Jackson Bate, Keats's biographer, puts the point this way:

> It is because 'To Autumn' is so uniquely a distillation, and at many different levels, that each generation has found it one of the most nearly perfect poems in English. We need not be afraid of continuing to use the adjective. In its strict sense the word is peculiarly applicable: the whole is 'perfected' — carried through to completion — solely by means of the given parts; and the parts observe decorum ... by contributing directly to the whole, with nothing left dangling or independent.
>
>   (*John Keats*, Harvard, 1963)

I think that this perfection might be accounted for by the hypothesis that Keats has gone firmly over to an eroticism based on fulfilment. The addressee of the poem, Autumn, is the season and also, by personification, a unique individual female, like Isabella or Lamia or Madeline. As female, her main attribute in the first stanza is caring maternalism. She is the season of 'mellow fruitfulness', who, as 'bosom friend' of the sun 'conspires' with him — and in context, the word may connote sexual union — to populate the world with fruit and flowers, in a sense, the offspring of autumn. In the second stanza, Autumn is no longer a specific and unique woman, but is dispersed into the various forms of autumnal labour: she is a granary worker, a reaper, a gleaner, a cider-maker. In each case, the work she does is not seen as destructive — even as a reaper, she is prey to sensuality and this has the effect of sparing the environment and her own 'twined flowers'. A recent critic, Richard Rand, in a very provocative essay simply called '"O'er brimm'd"', points out that the various female figures in this stanza are recastings of other Keatsian women, so that, for example, Autumn asleep on the 'half-reap'd furrow' is a version of Madeline's much less productive sleep when the 'poppied warmth of sleep oppress'd/ Her soothed limbs' (ll.237–238); while the image of the gleaner is a celebratory rewriting of the desolate image of Ruth in the 'Ode to a Nightingale', 'when, sick for home,/ She stood in tears amid the alien corn' (ll.66–67). To me the final image of the stanza:

> Or by a cyder-press, with patient look,
> Thou watchest the last oozings hours by hours

is so perfect because it combines contemplation, watching, with a slow but very steady process of fruition. There is a marriage, in this image, of the two kinds of sexuality that I have suggested underlie some of Keats's major poems. Unlike Porphyro, whose watching of Madeline seems so unhealthily cut off from her, or our own isolated watching of the urn, Autumn here is witnessing one of her own processes, the distillation into cider of the life-giving juices that Autumn has put there is stanza 1. The poem ends with the composition of a symphony to Autumn, patterned out of the sounds of her own music.

AFTERTHOUGHTS

Explain why Hammond begins this essay with an account of Coleridge's 'Christabel'.

What do you understand by 'preferring the erotics of contemplation to the erotics of possession' (page 37)? Do you agree with Hammond's theory?

Compare Hammond's response to the rose imagery in 'The Eve of St Agnes' (pages 33, 34, 35) with Brooks-Davies's discussion of the same imagery in the next essay (pages 42–51).

Explain how Hammond relates his analysis of 'The Eve of St Agnes' to the other poems he considers in this essay.

Douglas Brooks-Davies
*Douglas Brooks-Davies is Senior
Lecturer in English Literature at the
University of Manchester, and author of
numerous critical studies.*

ESSAY

The two Marys in 'The Eve of St Agnes' — the place of Christian imagery in Keats's definition of love

'The Eve of St Agnes', with its slumbering maiden released from her enchantment by her lover, is fascinatingly similar to the fairy tale in which the Sleeping Beauty, Rosebud, is wakened from her hundred-years' sleep by a kiss from the prince who, like Porphyro, reaches the girl only after overcoming formidable obstacles. Porphyro has to find his way through the forbidding maze of the parental castle; the prince has to force his way through thorn thickets that turn into roses at his approach. The similarity, though probably coincidental, is instructive. Roses are named four times in Keats's poem (stanzas XVI, XXV, XXVII, XXXVI) in connection with the burning (stanzas IX, XVIII) lover and his beloved. If Keats is arguing, as T S Eliot was to write in one of his *Four Quartets* a century or so later with the full force of Christian and other mysticisms behind him, that 'the fire and the rose are one' (end of 'Little Gidding'), then we need to ask how he conveys this idea in the poem, how he persuades us of the nature and rightness of the union between Porphyro and his rose queen.

The answer is that the rose guides us to the figures and mythologies of the two Marys, the Virgin Mother of God and St Mary Magdalen, the reformed prostitute who entered Christian thinking as the result of slightly obscure references in Luke 7 and 8 and Mark 16. The Virgin Mary is, in Catholic tradition, the mystic rose (in part because of Song of Solomon 2:1, 'I am the rose of Sharon') and both she and her rosary guard the threshold of the poem in stanza I where the Beadsman tells his beads and his breath rises 'past the sweet Virgin's picture'. It is Mary Magdalen, however, who is the poem's central figure, for she is commemorated in the form of Madeline, whose name derives directly from Magdalen, as the cancelled stanza VIa announced unequivocally when it said that the girl dreaming under the influence of the St Agnes legend would wake 'Warm in the virgin morn, no weeping Magdalen'.

Later, at stanza XXV, rose, as both flower and colour, links the two Marys when the Virgin's rose transmits its hues onto the praying Madeline–Magdalen: 'Rose-bloom fell on her hands'. Yet Porphyro, too, is not only burning but rosy: 'Sudden a thought came like a full-blown rose,/ Flushing his brow' (ll.136–137). And his name, wisely changed from the first draft's Lionel, emphasises his burning rosiness by deriving from Greek *porphyros* (purple). He is rosy and purple because he is the active agent in a world that is otherwise dark, wintry, and regressively dormant. He is the means through which the Virgin's rose will be transformed into the rose of fiery erotic passion. What the poem portrays, I shall argue, is the substitution of the one rose for the other, Porphyro's for Mary's, as Madeline is liberated from her state of virginity (stanza XXXVI). Why, though, should the Magdalen be so crucial to Keats's argument?

The reasons are, first, that Keats was himself in love and thus presumably felt an urgent personal irritation with the concept of virginity; second, that he rejected Christianity as superstition of a morbid and pernicious kind; and third — the product of the previous two — that he found the prevailing polarisation of woman into virgin and whore (itself rooted in the misogyny of the Church Fathers and endorsed by centuries of

Christian patriarchy) repellent. The Magdalen is central here as Christianity's exemplary penitant whore, the sinner who gave her name to houses of correction for prostitutes (Keats's 'The House of Mourning written by Mr Scott' of April 1819 refers to 'a sermon at the Magdalen'), a woman who, was made a victim for her sexual awareness.

Like Michèle Roberts in her novel *The Wild Girl* (1984), then, Keats decided to attempt a revisionist myth of the Marys. 'The Eve of St Agnes' rejects the Virgin's virginity and relieves Mary Magdalen of the stain historically laid upon her. Madeline as the Magdalen is protrayed as a girl who is no sinner but, simply, an initiate into sexual mysteries. Christianity emerges from this poem as the enemy of the religion of love which Keats celebrates in, for example, the 'Ode to Psyche', and as the great proponent of superstition, the force which, through St Agnes and her patron of virginity the 'sweet Virgin' (the Virgin Mary), leads Madeline to sleep and dream and wish to be a rosebud rather than a rose-bloom (stanza XXVII). The rose prince opposes the mystic rose of Mary in order that the Magdalen may be redeemed from the ignominy cast on her by patriarchal ignorance, in order that the cultural memory of the Magdalen may be erased and the innocence of the girl Madeline exalted in her place.

As an aid to asserting the primacy of erotic love over Christianity's cult of virginity Keats gives the poem a medieval setting, locating it somewhere in the fourteenth century when the cult of the Virgin was at its height and had long informed the love plaints of the troubadours. Indeed, Porphyro plays a Provençal song which Keats, again in 1819, made his own, 'La Belle Dame sans Merci'; and Porphyro's action is relevant to the Mary theme not only because it emphasises the historical moment when sacred and profane love were, in poetry and painting, finely balanced one against the other, but also because Provence, in legend at least, saw the origin of Mary's rosary, that powerful meditative and penitential symbol through which we enter the poem.

At the opening the Beadsman is enacting the meaning of his name by bidding (praying) his beads. But his fingers are numb and the landscape so frozen that one doubts the efficacy of his prayers and that of the lady to whom he prays. For it is as if the Virgin, past whose icon his 'frosted breath' rises, has caused — or at least approves of — this icy desolation; as if she is a *dame sans merci* herself and the Beadsman her enthralled aged and pathetic lover.

The Beadsman is thus presented as the victim of Christianity's superstitions as they are expressed through the cult of Mary, just as Madeline is depicted as the victim of Agnes. Unlike Madeline, though, he is killed by his superstition. For when he has prayed his rosary he walks 'northward' towards the prospect of his death (stanza III) and, when we meet him again at the end of this circle of a poem, actually dies with the name of his Virgin on his lips: 'The Beadsman, after thousand aves told,/ For aye unsought for slept among his ashes cold' (ll.377–378).

The desolation and death endured by the Beadsman are exactly what Christianity represented to Keats in an earlier poem, 'Written in Disgust of Vulgar Superstition' (December 1816), where he had contrasted its tomb-like chill with a new religion symbolised by 'fresh flowers'. The 'fresh flower' in 'The Eve of St Agnes' is, of course, Porphyro, the Beadsman's opposite, the rose who penetrates the castle in order to displace the Virgin's rose with his own rose lady whom he then removes to a region that is at the furthest extreme from the Beadsman's deathly celibate north: 'o'er the southern moors I have a home for thee' (l.351). This region of fertility and life is the land of erotic union that has, in fact, already been described in terms of flowers at the moment of Madeline's and Porphyro's lovemaking:

> Into her dream he melted, as the rose
> Blendeth its odour with the violet, —
> Solution sweet . . .

> (ll.320–322)

The language has a haunting grammatical ambiguity here, for 'rose' and 'violet' function as noun and adjective simultaneously and, in breaking out of the straitjacket of grammatical categories, seem to be attempting to mine the transcendence of spatial limitation achieved by the lovers as spirit blends with spirit in counterpoint to and contradiction of the frozen incense of the Beadsman's breath in stanza I. But these lines gain added point if we acknowledge the extent of Porphyro's appropriation of imagery associated with Mary. It is this blend of odours, not the pious breath of the Beadsman, that recalls the 'pillars of smoke, perfumed with myrrh and frankincense' of Song of Solomon 3:6 — an image that was again applied to the Virgin. And the blend has been achieved through the combination of Porphyro's fiery non-Marian rose with Madeline's violet, a flower which Marian iconography borrowed from imagery associated with Venus. The result is a 'solution' of two in one that represents the essence of Keats's religion of love and that depends upon the transference of Marian symbols to a pair of lovers whose purity, Keats indicates here, outstrips that traditionally accorded to the Virgin, or at least equals it.

This union in terms of rose and violet — the climax of the poem — is prepared for by two earlier moments, that in which Madeline kneels before the stained-glass window, and Porphyro's preparation of the feast in her bedchamber. Both demand explication in terms of imagery associated with Mary.

The magnificent set-piece description of the window has a remarkable symbolic density:

> A casement high and triple-arched there was,
> All garlanded with carven imag'ries
> Of fruits, and flowers, and bunches of knot-grass,
> And diamonded with panes of quaint device,
> Innumerable of stains and splendid dyes,
> As are the tiger-moth's deep-damask'd wings;
> And in the midst, 'mong thousand heraldries,
> And twilight saints, and dim emblazonings,
> A shielded scutcheon blush'd with blood of queens and kings.
>
> Full on this casement shone the wintry moon,
> And threw warm gules on Madeline's fair breast,
> As down she knelt for heaven's grace and boon;
> Rose-bloom fell on her hands, together prest,
> And on her silver cross soft amethyst,
> And on her hair a glory, like a saint
>
> (stanzas XXIV–XXV)

The red 'scutcheon' will, as a result of the love-making between Porphyro and Madeline, be transformed into another icon of that love, 'Thy beauty's shield, heart-shap'd and vermeil dyed', Porphyro himself (1.336), now, as at the beginning ('with heart on fire', 1.75), a passionately erotic version of Christ as redeemer, the merciful discloser of the Sacred Heart. Here as elsewhere, in other words, Porphyro invests with the life of erotic love, symbols that Keats felt to be culturally dead. How, though, does the rest of the window episode relate to the poem as I have been describing it?

The first thing to notice is that we are being confronted with a power struggle between opposed forces which has Madeline as its focus: on the one hand the moon and the window; in the centre Madeline; on the other hand Porphyro, who has hidden in her chamber with the help of Angela. Notice, too, that the window is red and purple (blood, gules, rose-bloom, amethyst), that is, the same colours as those embodied in Porphyro and in the union of rose and violet in stanza XXXVI. The moon is complemented by Angela, then, and the window by Porphyro to produce this symmetrical tableau:

moon/ window // Madeline // Porphyro/ Angela

And what the moon does is, against the laws of light, optics, and whatever, to project the window's colours onto Madeline.

The point is that the moon is the planet of virginity. Dedicated by the Romans to the virgin goddess Diana, it found its way into Marian iconography via Song of Solomon 6:10 ('Who is she that looketh forth as the morning, fair as the moon . . .?') and Revelation 12:1 ('And there appeared a great wonder in heaven; a woman clothed with the sun, and the moon under her feet'), both of which verses were understood as describing Mary. The moon of the Virgin which is also the moon of the virgin martyr Agnes ('St Agnes' moon hath set', 1.324) thus shines through the window in order to claim Madeline for the regressive forces of Christianity. As it shines she takes on the hues of the Marian rose and her cross glows with the colour of Christ's blood, while the window itself, with its heraldic shields and saints, encodes exactly those forces of aristocratic privilege and religious conspiracy that the castle as a whole represents and which Porphyro is dedicated to destroying.

Porphyro stands for the same colours but with the opposite meaning. He watches, waiting to project his own rose bloom on her, to erase the stain left by the window. And it is the fact that he has reached Madeline with Angela's help that turns him into something more than a Peeping Tom with nothing better to do than spy on adolescent girls as they undress. For Angela is rather mysterious. Her name says that she is a messenger, an intermediary, an *angelos*. She is aged and is credited with magical powers (stanza XV); she has a stick that is again mysteriously magical: an 'ivory-headed wand' (l.92). If she helps Porphyro she must oppose the virginal moon; simultaneously, though, she shares Madeline's (and the moon goddess's) gender.

She is, in fact, that familiar romance figure, the wise woman with her distaff, personification of the powers of Hecate, goddess of enchantment who is the archetypal aged crone and who signifies the moon below the horizon, the moon in her dark phase. Ancient, dark, and feminine, she has a phasal — indeed, a maternal — relationship with her moon daughter whom, as an aspect of herself, she guides through the various stages of her life-cycle — childhood virginity, pubertal awakening, childbirth and motherhood, and death. She is the old woman who, in some versions of *Sleeping Beauty*, enables the prince to waken Rosebud. As messenger and transmitter of the powers of female growth, she has exactly this function in 'The Eve of St Agnes', though in the poem the symbolism is even more precise. She negates the moon of the virgin phase which possesses Madeline by colouring her with the 'rose-bloom' of Marian virginity, and introduces rosy-purple Porphyro in its place. As confirmation of this interpretation, note how the mullion — carved with the 'fruits, and flowers, and bunches of knot-grass' of the earth mother Demeter–Ceres which were, again, assimilated into the cult of the Virgin — is displaced by Porphyro's feast of real, life-giving, edible fruit. In comparison with these, the carved fruit is like (because it belongs to the same world as) the 'sculptur'd dead' of stanza II.

Stanza XXV marks the transition to the feast episode. Madeline has finished her evening prayers, 'her vespers' (but *Vesper* is *Hesper*, the evening star, which is also the morning star and planet Venus; the Virgin Mary is also the morning star), removes the garlands of pearl from her hair (pearl garlands complement the Virgin's rosary, since pearls, because of their colour and shape, were dedicated to the moon as planetary deity of virginity; the Virgin is often adorned with pearls), then unveils her body so that she appears 'half-hidden, like a mermaid in sea-weed'. The cancelled reading 'Syren of the sea' was much too sexually explicit and tonally inaccurate, for 'mermaid', like 'vespers', conjures up exactly the transitional quality that Angela is, through Porphyro's gazing eyes, willing upon Madeline: *mer-maid* suggests those puns on the Virgin's name that have delighted her devotees through the centuries (the troubadour fondness for punning (*mére* (mother), *mare* (sea), *marier* (to marry), for example). Madeline, as a virgin about to encounter the sexual awareness of a Magdalen without the stigma hagiolatry attaches to that particular saint, is at once a Mary-maid and a sea (*mer*) maid, a creature of the ocean like Venus, goddess of erotic love, who was herself born from the sea.

Then, as she sleeps, Porphyro arranges the feast, spicy and strange with its 'quince, and plum, and gourd', its 'lucent syrops, tinct with cinnamon'; its 'Manna and dates, in argosy transferr'd/ From Fez; and spiced dainties, every one,/ From silken Samarcand to cedar'd Lebanon' (stanza XXX). 'Manna' is biblical, a gift from God to the Israelites (Exodus 16:15); and cedars of Lebanon are Old Testament biblical as well. In fact, as we read that these 'delicates' fill Madeline's room with their perfume (stanza XXXI) we begin to sense an echo of an Old Testament book that I have alluded to in passing more than once in this essay, the Song of Solomon, and specifically chapter 4:11–14:

> Thy lips, O my spouse, drop as the honeycomb: honey and milk are under thy tongue; and the smell of thy garments is like the smell of Lebanon.
>
> A garden inclosed is my sister, my spouse; a spring shut up, a fountain sealed.
>
> Thy plants are an orchard of pomegranates, with pleasant fruits; camphire, with spikenard,
>
> Spikenard and saffron; calamus and cinnamon, with all trees of frankincense; myrrh and aloes, with all the chief spices.

The feel of Porphyro's feast addressed to Madeline, whom he now bids 'awake!', is identical to this (and indeed other) passages in the Song as the female and male lovers hymn each other antiphonally with images from a beautiful and fertile nature expressing love and loss that are among the most haunting in the Bible. And if we doubt that Keats does have the Song in mind, all we have to do is turn to the end of the poem where Porphyro again, and for the last time, urges Madeline 'Arise — arise! . . . Let us away, my love, with happy speed . . . Awake! arise! my love' (stanza XXXIX), because this echoes Song of Solomon 2:10–13:

> My beloved spake, and said unto me, Rise up, my
> fair one, and come away.
> For, lo, the winter is past, the rain is over and
> gone;
> The flowers appear on the earth; the time of the
> singing of birds is come. . .
> Arise, my love, my fair one, and come away.

Porphyro even adopts the repetitive structure of the original (arise . . . arise), and with his echo of the fervency of the Song we have reached our final clue to Keats's rewriting of the legends and attributes of the two Marys. For the Song, as I suggested earlier, is one of the main sources of Marian iconography: black Madonnas, the Virgin as the moon, the Virgin as an army with banners, the Virgin as an enclosed garden — these and many more originate in its eight short chapters. But, and this is the crux, the Song is actually a secular work, a celebration of erotic love in the form of a collection of love songs. It was attributed to King Solomon and found its way into the Wisdom books of the Old Testament, but Jewish and Christian theologians were always unhappy about it and felt obliged to allegorise it. Christian orthodoxy therefore turned it into the story of the church-bride's search for her bridegroom, Christ.

Eighteenth-century and romantic scepticism, however, spotted the erotic truth, and nineteenth-century biblical scholarship proved it. Hence in Thomas Hardy's novel *Jude the Obscure* (1895) Sue Bridehead was enabled to say to Jude: 'people have no right to falsify the Bible! I *hate* such humbug as could attempt to plaster over with ecclesiastical abstractions such ecstatic, natural, human love as lies in that great and passionate song!'

Keats, as 'Written in Disgust at Vulgar Superstition' shows, hated that kind of humbug too, and so with Porphyro's feast and his 'awake! arise!', he repossesses the Song for erotic love, relieving it of its burden of 'ecclesiastical abstraction'. His use of the Song is thus part of the poem's larger concern, which is to move Madeline from the protection of the 'sweet Virgin' through the agencies of the old crone Angela and of Porphyro so that she may become a sexual initiate, a Magdalen who, because she has been removed from the repressive forces of Christianity as exemplified in the cults of the two Marys, need feel no shame, need offer no repentance, for her sexual awakening. Angela, like the 'sweet Virgin', is left behind at the end because both mothers have been superseded by their symbolic daughter whose duty it has been to outgrow them. Madeline's journey south, 'o'er the southern moors', removes her from their and the Beadsman's land of death not just because it is the opposite of the 'northward' of stanza 3 but because it revives the erotic spirit of 'come, thou south [wind]; blow upon my garden, that the spices thereof may flow out' (Song of Solomon 4:16). Indeed, the union of scents described in stanza XXXVI originates here and not in any sexual coyness on Keats's part, and this means that Porphyro's journey from the castle to the garden leads him not just to that rose-violet Madeline, but to the mythical roots of the Virgin cult where the erotic and the sacral are one.

AFTERTHOUGHTS

1

Do you agree that Porphyro is a better name for Keats's hero than Lionel (see page 43)?

2

Who are the two Marys considered in this essay? Explain their importance, in Brooks-Davies's view, to Keats's portrayal of Madeline.

3

Does Brooks-Davies convince you that the Song of Solomon is a significant source for 'The Eve of St Agnes' (pages 49–51)?

4

Compare Brooks-Davies's response to the poem's rose imagery with Hammond's response to the same imagery in the previous essay (pages 33–35)

Peter Hollindale

Peter Hollindale is Senior Lecturer in
English and Education at the University
of York. He is General Editor of the
Macmillan Shakespeare, and has
produced numerous books and articles.

ESSAY

Romantic escape and corrective truth in Keats's odes and narrative poems

At the centre of Keats's imaginative achievement lie eight major poems. They are the five great odes ('Ode to a Nightingale', 'Ode on a Grecian Urn', 'Ode to Psyche', 'To Autumn' and 'Ode on Melancholy') and three narrative poems, 'Lamia', 'Isabella', and 'The Eve of St Agnes'). One other great poem, 'La Belle Dame sans Merci', is directly relevant to the following discussion, and may be found to represent in vivid miniature the theme and poetic structure which I shall be considering. However, it is excluded from full treatment here because its brief, restrained, ballad-like form raises different questions from those which arise in extended narrative, and I have taken the difference of form to override a similarity of experience and ideas. The two versions of 'Hyperion' are also omitted because, despite their wealth of interest, they remain no more than tantalising fragments, and it will be seen that the argument I shall hope to present can only be applied to completed works.

The five odes and two of the three long narrative poems were all written within the space of a year. The third, 'Isabella', was written some months earlier. Because of this concentrated period of composition, we might reasonably expect to find similarities of interest, theme or mood between them, however unique and distinctive each individual poem may be.

But the two groups are very different in their nature. The odes are poems of imaginative meditation, exploring the poet's reactions to intense contemplation of an object, a creature, a mythical goddess or a psychological condition, and all they signify for the writer in helping him to understand his own predicament as a human being and an artist. To all appearances, they are *static* poems. The narrative group, being stories, seem likely to be more *dynamic* in presentation and less preoccupied with the feeling and situation of Keats himself. Usually the eight works are discussed either as single poems or as two separate groups. I want to suggest that if we consider all of them together, we can find important similarities not only in their ideas but, more surprisingly, in their structure and shape. The odes are more dramatic than they seem, so that their construction and movement reflect a development of thoughts and emotions, while the narrative poems are more static than we expect, subordinating the flow of story to a single, central experience.

The characteristic pattern is easiest to see in the narrative poems. At the heart of each story is a secret: a secret love affair which happens in a secret place. Lamia and Lycius dwell together in a magically created palace in the middle of Corinth. When the 'gossip rout' arrives, foolishly summoned by Lycius to his catastrophic marriage feast, no one can remember seeing it before:

> The herd approach'd; each guest, with busy brain,
> Arriving at the portal, gaz'd amain,
> And enter'd marveling: for they knew the street,
> Remember'd it from childhood all complete
> Without a gap, yet ne'er before had seen
> That royal porch, that high-built fair demesne.
>
> ('Lamia' Part II, ll.150–155)

Madeline's chamber in 'The Eve of St Agnes' is another secret place. It is not illusory, as Lamia's mansion is, but it is an intimate, secluded, warm haven at the heart of a cold, inhos-

pitable castle. Isabella and Lorenzo meet out of doors, but still
in a place shut off from all intruders:

> Close in a bower of hyacinth and musk,
> Unknown of any, free from whispering tale.
>
> ('Isabella', stanza XI)

In all three poems the love affair is an illicit one, fraught
with danger if the outside world should discover it. The three
pairs of lovers are all breaking rules of custom and convention,
reaching out for a special intensity of love and pleasure which
exposure will destroy. For one reason or another, they are all
in a very similar plight to Shakespeare's Romeo and Juliet. The
parallel is closest for Porphyro and Madeline, who are divided
just as Romeo and Juliet are by family and tribal feuding.
Isabella and Lorenzo are publicly separated by differences of
wealth and status, and Lamia and Lycius by a strong taboo on
love between the mortal and the immortal. In each poem,
although both the lovers are offending against tyrannical
prohibitions and are both at risk, it is the man who has ventured
into forbidden territory. This is true even for Lycius, whose
mansion of love is at the heart of his own city.

The outside world is hostile and threatening in every
instance. In 'The Eve of St Agnes' and 'Lamia', the world from
which the lovers are insecurely hidden is a crowded and popu-
lous one, and no less threatening because its heart is set on
barbaric music and revelry. For both these secret celebrations
of love the voice of danger is the voice of music: in 'Lamia' it
is 'a thrill of trumpets' which wakens Lycius from his seclusion,
and in 'The Eve of St Agnes' the 'silver, snarling trumpets',
followed later by 'the kettle-drum, and far-heard clarinet'
betoken the festive banquet, which Porphyro's mortal enemies
are holding. Porphyro and Madeline, meanwhile, have their own
more delicate banquet, and the gentler music of Porphyro's lute.
In 'Isabella' the exterior threat is not a crowded public gathering: it is confined to Isabella's murderous brothers. But there
is still a contrasting world. The brothers have their own secrecy
and seclusion, focused not on love but on ledgers and money, and
it spreads out to a debased wide world of merchandise and
exploitation.

Particularly in 'Lamia' and 'The Eve of St Agnes' (but also

hinted at in stanza XI of 'Isabella') the meeting-place of love and its fulfilment is marked not only by extraordinary intensity of passionate feeling, but also by a kind of ritual stillness and trance-like delight. Mutterings from the excluded busy world perhaps break in, as does the 'boisterous, midnight, festive clarion' on Madeline and Porphyro, and the poet may have warned us of secrecy and risk, but the climax of hidden passion seems briefly immune from the ordinary rules of time. It has a different dimension, like a dream. In 'Lamia', the effect is achieved with astonishing brevity:

> . . . side by side
> They were enthroned, in the even tide,
> Upon a couch, near to a curtaining
> Whose airy texture, from a golden string,
> Floated into the room, and let appear
> Unveil'd the summer heaven, blue and clear,
> Betwixt two marble shafts: — there they reposed,
> Where use had made it sweet, with eyelids closed,
> Saving a tythe which love still open kept,
> That they might see each other while they almost slept'
>
> (Part II, ll.16–25)

As soon as the spell is broken, however, we become aware of tension, agitation and haste: the patter of wind-blown sleet stirs Porphyro and Madeline to urgent escape; Lorenzo is hustled away at short notice by the murderous brothers; Lycius hastens to summon his disruptive friends. The effect is to place the secret experience of love at the very heart of the poem, transcending everything else in value, putting life on a different plane, but also fragile and vulnerable. In their different ways, each of the three poems shows the approach to love, holds it at the centre, and causes the external world to break it up.

In the odes the centres of interest are very different, but in most cases the *structure* is remarkably similar. (The exception is the 'Ode to Psyche', which has a quite separate but equally satisfying pattern.) What we find in each case is an opening phase which prepares the way for an intense central experience, comparable to that of love. The preparatory phase essentially has one of two forms. In the first, it gradually approaches a core of intensity, moving closer and building concentration from a beginning in contemplative quietness. In the second form, Keats begins with the fact of intense, heightened experience, and rejects possible ways of making its intensity less conscious and therefore more endurable; instead, he chooses to accept the intensity, and to experience greater joy even if this inevitably means that he will also experience pain.

The first of these two forms is represented in the 'Ode on a Grecian Urn' and 'To Autumn'. The opening stanza of the 'Ode on a Grecian Urn' begins quietly, and its subject is quietness; it begins in still, observant meditation, and its subject is stillness; it begins slowly, and its subject is slowness. Keats, very much the self-conscious poet, is looking at a work of art which can outdo poetry itself. As his observant eye closes in on the story depicted in the details of the urn's frieze, all these initial qualities give way. His questions, as he looks more and more closely, become increasingly excited. Quietness gives way to sound ('pipes and timbrels'); stillness and slowness give way to movement and speed ('mad pursuit'; 'struggle to escape'): the poet and story-teller is absorbed in someone else's story. The way is prepared for the ecstatic, idealised but precarious vision of the three central stanzas.

'To Autumn' also begins quietly, in a mood of descriptive stillness, with the poet as a detached and serene observer. Many critics suggest that this is all he is, throughout. A little later I want to suggest a different way of looking at this poem. For the moment, the point to stress is the gradual closing-in during the first stanza on smaller and nearer details of autumnal fruitfulness, and along with it the movement and activity of ripening which Keats records: the self-enriching process of abundant harvest and fruition. Here too the poet is preparing the way, this time for the still centrepiece of the second stanza.

The second introductory form in the odes, which begins with alternative responses to heightened experience, is fairly simply represented by 'Ode on Melancholy'. The first stanza is a dismissal of one possible reaction to the experience of melancholy ('go not to Lethe'). It is a cumulative rejection of diminished consciousness: Keats is turning away from the escapist consolations of death, narcotic slumber, drugged unconsciousness, forgetfulness. By turning aside from the lure of sedation Keats prepares the way for the opposite response in the second stanza, where melancholy is turned face to face with objects which ought to arouse joy, and are therefore likely to make the experience of melancholy even more painful than it was. These are imagined moments of heightened consciousness, and their complex, contradictory, paradoxical nature leads in turn to the third stanza's assertion of the close kinship between melancholy and joy, pain and pleasure, the transience of life and its keen intensity.

'Ode to a Nightingale' is a more complex poem, but a simple outline of its structure may show that it too follows the essential pattern of 'Ode on Melancholy'. At the start of the poem Keats is already expressing the almost unbearable severity of extreme happiness induced by the nightingale's song. His first impulse is again towards a painless loss of consciousness through joy, as if the bird's song were acting as a friendly poison or anaesthetic drug. The second stanza is tempted by a similar forgetfulness, this time through intoxication as wine and birdsong lull the senses. Each lapse of consciousness is a way of escaping the fact of worldly suffering and mortality depicted in the third stanza. But just as the 'Ode on Melancholy' turned in its second stanza from unconsciousness to the intensities of painful joy, so this poem turns in its fourth stanza from the happiness of luxurious exhaustion to the happiness of sharpened awareness, from experiencing the nightingale's forest in a soothing coma to experiencing it in sensuously alerted wakefulness. And — significantly not only for this poem but for all Keats's work — the agent of this change is poetry itself, and the act of writing it: wine is replaced by 'the viewless wings of poesy'.

This tension between two kinds of escape — escape into unconsciousness and escape into painful acceptance of intenser life — is replayed for a second time in the poem, as Keats in stanza 6 surrenders in imagination to the seductive peace of death, and then in stanza 7 recoils from it. But the process of rejection is what matters, and the second movement of the poem reaffirms the first. The choice of heightened life, the repudiation of painless narcotic escape, is witnessed by the fact of the poetry itself. The very act of writing poetry becomes fused with the choices the poet is making. At the centre of the ode is a strong visionary experience, and yet it is one which lies outside the norms and truths of everyday life. Like all visionary experience, it cannot last, and the final stanza records the poet's return to normal consciousness, and his uncertainty about what has happened.

Both 'Ode on Melancholy' and 'Ode to a Nightingale', then, present a central visionary experience which is intense, and placed somewhere outside the usual dimensions of time, somewhere in 'imaginative time', by its vividness and significance. But usual time and usual experience inevitably supersede it. The closing stanzas act as a second and corrective truth to the visionary truth of sorrows glutted on joy, or the nightingale's song. They acknowledge the instability of imaginative vision, and the other, inescapable truth of reality, what Keats termed 'Misery and Heartbreak, Pain, Sickness and oppression'.

If we look back to the first two odes discussed here, 'Ode on a Grecian Urn' and 'To Autumn', I think we shall find that they structure experience in much the same way. In the central stanzas of 'Ode on a Grecian Urn', Keats is contemplating an apparent visionary solution to the problems of time and mortality, finding it in the permanence of art. But as he re-creates the captive, frozen, joyous moments of the urn's arrested story, his candid vision is forced to accept its inadequacy as an ideal. Its permanent life is won at the cost of permanent unfulfilment, its vivid sculptured happenings in one place must be paid for by eternal absence from another. In the last stanza he is forced to withdraw from visionary intensity and return to the pleased but meditative distance where he started. It is the urn itself — 'Cold Pastoral', with all that the phrase implies — which offers consoling delight, not the life it depicts. It offers beauty and pleasure, but not escape. The visionary centre has rich imaginative value, but is incomplete without the distancing corrective truth of the closing lines.

About 'To Autumn' there is more to be said, but at this point I would simply suggest that the perfect, poised seasonal stillness of the second stanza gives way in the third to recognition that the year moves on, the swallows migrate, the year inevitably turns towards winter. The reality of the seasonal cycle is fully registered, and the momentary illusion of permanence is corrected, in the dynamic movement of the closing stanza.

If we are to describe these poems as 'escapist', therefore, the word must be strictly qualified. In all the poems it seems that Keats is looking for some experience or image which will suspend the process of age, time and decay, weariness, pain and loss, and carry him through the act of poetic imagination into a vision which combines intense joy with stability and peace. In the narrative poems it is the experience of secret human love; in the odes it is an image which brings into some kind of synthesis the contradictory states of time and permanence. Essentially the interest, the object of his search, is the same in both groups of poems. (If we accept the role played by the poetic imagination — which is not only a means to an end but a part of the accomplished permanence he hopes for — the pattern also includes 'Ode to Psyche', which celebrates the poet's power to integrate warm human emotion with the immortality of a goddess.) And if the objective is essentially the same, so is the structure. There is an approach, where the lovers move tentatively, daringly and riskily towards a meeting, or the poet moves towards a full encounter with his central image. There is a middle section, in the narrative poems a climax, perhaps very brief, of hidden love and sexual consummation, and in the odes of intense, ecstatic contemplation of the chosen image, reaching out towards timeless joy. Finally there is (almost everywhere except in the 'Ode to Psyche') a closing phase which disperses the brief ecstasy. In the narrative poems love is killed or forced to flee. In the odes the poet is called back from contemplation of his central image to recognise the fact of time and transience, and realise that the earlier image is incomplete.

In this pattern there is certainly a need for escape, but it cannot be written off as 'escapism'. Keats is not a fugitive; he is an explorer. The poetic ventures of these poems start from a base-camp in the painful realities of living, and they return there when they must. It is not a question of trying to replace truth by illusion. Instead we realise that there are two kinds of truth. The experience of a mountaineer on the summit he has scaled is not the same as his experience in the everyday world: it is more intense and exhilarating but also more short-lived. But *both* experiences are real, and true. The contrary experiences of Keats's great poems can be understood in much the same way. One poet's imagination, like one climber's personality, is the meeting-place for two kinds of truth. What Keats is seeking is an event or image which will resolve the tension between them, and integrate them in one single experience. The 'corrective' truth at the end of the poem does not devalue the vision at its centre, but it may show with painful honesty how far apart they are.

Sometimes the tension between contradictory, even opposite truths is contained in the central image. When Keats cries out to the nightingale:

> Thou wast not born for death, immortal Bird!
>   No hungry generations tread thee down

(ll.61–62)

he is not speaking to the individual bird, which is mortal like himself. He is speaking of the song, which stays the same with every generation of nightingales, as if it were an abstract and stable object of beauty, like a work of art. But the nightingale he is hearing is a living thing, and disappears into the next valley. The image will not sustain the demands he is placing on it, and the poem's final stanza is a courageous acceptance of uncertainty. The 'Ode on a Grecian Urn' is an effort to reach synthesis from the opposite direction, with the work of art as its starting point. But once again the attempted integration is a failure. In bringing to imagined life the idealised youthful figures on the urn, Keats is inescapably confronted with the frustration, loss and unfulfilment which is the price of their eternal stasis. Again, the central image will not provide the hoped-for fusion, and a momentary rapture of illusion is corrected by imaginative truth.

In these instances the failure of the image does not mean that the poem itself fails. These are great odes, in part because of the very completeness with which they express the poet's imaginative ambition and its limits. Their strains and tensions are part of their greatness. The strains are also evident in the narrative poems, but here the damage to their poetic coherence can be greater. 'Isabella', in particular, must be counted as a failure. Keats himself thought little of it ('A weak-sided Poem', he called it, 'with an amusing sober-sadness about it'), and it has numerous local mishaps of taste, style and tone. Yet there are few poems in the language which show greater promise, and Keats deserves more credit than is usually given for the dramatic balance between the secret ceremony of love, life and joy in the first half of the poem and of love, death and grief in the second. In 'Lamia', a more mature and accomplished poem, the tensions are even more apparent, above all when Lycius (with the poet's evident sympathy) denounces the philosopher Apollonius for a series of wrongs which are actually true of Lamia herself. (See 'Lamia' Part 2, ll. 277–290.)

In these poems we can see a persistent sense on Keats's part of truths which seem contrary yet are very close together, the truths of poetic imagination and those of observable reality. Again and again, at crucial points, they meet: sleep and waking, dream-visions and waking dreams; pain and pleasure; unconsciousness and heightened consciousness; transience and permanence; philosophic truth and poetic truth; thought and sensation; poetry itself and the things it celebrates.

The narrative poem in which Keats came closest to achieving a satisfactory fusion between idealised secret love and mortal life is 'The Eve of St Agnes'. Of that larger effort to find a completely satisfying image which integrates movement and stillness, time and eternity, mortality and immortality, we can say that he did finally achieve what he was seeking. 'To Autumn' is the perfect expression of a perfect image. We have already looked at the gradual approach to self-enriching fruition in the opening stanza of this poem. In the second stanza, and apart from one small reference *only* in the second stanza, Autumn is personified as a figure, both deity and human being. The figure is characterised by attitudes of extreme stillness, 'sitting careless on a granary floor', 'sound asleep':

> And sometimes like a gleaner thou dost keep
> Steady thy laden head across a brook;
> Or by a cyder-press, with patient look,
> Thou watchest the last oozings hours by hours.

It is impossible to separate mortal from immortal in this stanza, or time from timelessness. Yet in the third stanza the personified figure recedes, and the processes of time, change and death resume their course as the yearly cycle turns towards winter. In this case, however, the image is flawless. Unlike the urn, Autumn is a living thing, made up of growth and decay and the process of organic life; unlike the nightingale it does not die, but recurs and recurs in the ceaseless turning of the years. The season is drowsy and wakeful; joyful and sad. For Keats the image is completely expressive of what he wished to find and to say: it exhibits no strains or tensions, and requires no thought, no philosophic intrusion outside itself. But that is not to say that it is merely 'descriptive', or that it expresses no ideas. On the contrary, it is a formidably intelligent poem, a fusion of idea, image and expression. Like great music, what it says is completely contained in what it is. In this poem the truth of romantic vision and the truth of reality are finally made one.

AFTERTHOUGHTS

1

What distinctions does Hollindale draw in this essay between the odes and the narrative poems?

2

What *is* the pattern of 'Ode to Psyche' (page 56)? Do you agree that it is 'equally satisfying' in comparison with the other poems under discussion?

3

Compare Hollindale's analysis of 'To Autumn' (pages 62–63) with Creaser's essay (pages 113–123).

4

What do you understand by 'escapist' (page 59)? What arguments does Hollindale put forward to defend Keats from the charge of escapism? Is escapism necessarily bad?

Ian Haywood

*Ian Haywood has extensive experience of
teaching English Literature in a variety
of educational establishments. He has
recently published* Faking It *(Harvester,
1986).*

ESSAY

Desire and denial in the odes and other poems

This essay will argue that desire is one of the most powerful impulses behind Keats's poetry. Moreover, it will be seen that both the frustration and granting of desire create some of the profoundest effects of the major poems.

To substantiate this ambitious claim it is necessary first of all to consider the nature of desire. For desire to exist at all there must be something to be desired: a goal, objective or result which will enhance or improve one's position in some way. It is possible of course to desire something to happen to someone else, but desire is most commonly related to one's own needs, dreams and fantasies.

In Keats's poems there are two ways in which desire is conspicuously revealed. Firstly, many poems contain the 'confessional' or personal outpourings of the poet. The poet speaks directly to the reader about his feelings. Secondly, the poems often have another focus: descriptions, images, themes, incidents. To make the distinction between these two 'levels' clear, we can look briefly at how they are present in 'Ode to a Nightingale'. 'O, for a draught of vintage!' (l.11) is clearly the 'confessional' level. The poet would like to be in a state of real or metaphorical intoxication ('vintage' refers to vintage wine) that will enable him to 'leave the world unseen' (l.19). The second level of desire is manifested later in the poem in the description of the biblical character Ruth. Her 'sad heart' is 'sick for home' (l.66). Her feelings are her own, not the poet's.

There is also a third and less accessible level of desire. This concerns the role of poetry and the imagination in supplying satisfaction. I will look at this type of desire first because it is difficult and requires elaboration, but it is also crucial to an understanding of Keats.

Keats's own term for the imagination was 'fancy'. He wrote an important poem with that title. One might be tempted to overlook 'Fancy'. It seems at first sight a light and playful poem, but its alluring and appetising descriptions actually constitute the evidence of the poem's argument, which is that 'sweet Fancy' can satisfy all our fantasies. The poem claims there is a need to liberate fancy because 'at home' in the normal, imperfect world, 'At a touch sweet Pleasure melteth', 'Summer's joys are spoilt by use', and it is impossible to find a 'cheek that doth not fade,/ Too much gaz'd at'. These generalisations about the fleeting nature of gratification are developed and explored in the odes. Rather like a magic genie, fancy can provide superior pleasure without the need for us to move an inch. Fancy's riches are not 'spoilt by use' because they are the intangible creations of the imagination. Rather than one season giving way to another the fancy can bring to us the most appealing seasons (spring, summer, autumn) simultaneously, mixing them like three wines to be consumed. Most significantly, fancy can provide sexual stimulation. It can conjure 'a mistress to thy mind'. The concluding section of the poem needs close scrutiny. The assumption is that the reader is male, in need of a 'mistress' or female lover. We note that fancy is also female, as was traditionally the muse of poetry. So there are strong connections between male sexual desire, the imagination, and the creation of poetry, of which 'Fancy' is of course an example.

Mortal beauty withers quickly, so the ideal mistresses of the fancy are like goddesses: Proserpine (or Persephone) and Hebe. The mythological and classical allusions in Keats's poetry are often worth pursuing if one wishes to understand the complexities and layers of meaning. Proserpine, daughter of Ceres the goddess of harvests, was carried off to the underworld by Pluto and forced to become its queen. She had to spend half of each year there, and this time became associated with winter. Keats's poem, however, desires Proserpine before her rape and abduction, before the creation of the most inclement season (this accords with the middle section of the poem) and before she was forced to 'frown' and 'chide' at her position. Fancy can bring her virginal and untouched and therefore more desirable. Yet there is little to choose between this position and Pluto's. Remember the characteristic motion of fancy is a 'mysterious stealth'. We also think of the 'unravish'd' Grecian urn, and could also allude to a famous remark in a letter to Bailey of 22 November 1817 that 'What the imagination *seizes* as Beauty must be truth' (my italics). The implications are disturbing. The other immortal mistress is Hebe, the perpetually youthful servant of the gods. She was dismissed from her post for stumbling and accidentally exposing herself. Keats makes this moment of humiliation and embarrassment one of voyeuristic pleasure, focusing on 'when her zone/ Slipt its golden clasp, and down/ Fell her kirtle to her feet' (ll.85–87). Jove may have been languidly drunk, but the intention of the description is clearly erotic arousal. The poem does not allow the sexual desire to be gratified, but suspends it at its most powerful position, on the threshold. To deny the fulfilment is to intensify the desire. The sumptuous feast that Porphyro lays out in 'The Eve of St Agnes' is not meant to be eaten.

The mind which must liberate fancy if these pleasures are to be granted is described as 'self-overaw'd'. This intriguing epithet alerts us again to the possible pitfalls of Keats's position. The compound word has three units: 'awed', 'over', and 'self'. To be 'awed' is to be supremely moved by an experience. In Keats's day such a feeling would be called 'sublime'. To be 'overaw'd' is barely possible. It means the faculties are overloaded, over-burdened, glutted beyond the sublime. Moreover, this surfeit is possible without any outside stimulus: 'self-overaw'd'. This would seem to accord with a remark Keats made in a letter to Taylor, 27 February 1818, that 'Poetry should surprise by a fine excess'. Much depends on that fineness, because the 'excess' can easily become self-indulgence, an immature, regressive, unrestrained self-gratification. From this hostile viewpoint, much of the luscious, effusive sensuousness of the poetry is comparable to a child desiring candy. The contemporary satirical poet Lord Byron described Keat's poetry as 'onanism' or masturbation. That view is too reductive, and Byron was referring mainly to 'Endymion'. But the notion that each poem by Keats is another mind-mistress is a persuasive one. We can see this in a famous letter of October 1818 which initially seems to counter the allegation. Keats says that his 'poetical Character' is not egotistical: 'it is not itself — it has no self'. His poems therefore can hardly be his bursting joy's grape against his palate. But if he does not seek pleasure directly, his surrogate 'camelion' certainly does:

> . . . it enjoys light and shade; it lives in gusto, be it foul or fair, high or low, rich or poor, mean or elevated — It has as much delight in conceiving an Iago as an Imogen. What shocks the virtuous philoso[p]her delights the camelion Poet. It does no harm from its relish of the dark side of things any more than from its taste for the bright one. . .
>
> (letter to Woodhouse, 27 October 1818)

Allowing for an element of bravado, we can see why Wordsworth called Keats a pagan. Later in the letter Keats in fact resorts to more direct statement: 'I feel assured I should write from the mere yearning and fondness I have for the Beautiful'. 'I look upon fine Phrases like a Lover,' he said elsewhere. 'Look upon' can mean 'regard' and 'look at'. Both meanings are erotic; the latter is also voyeuristic. Keats (in the November 1817 letter to Bailey) compared the imagination famously to 'Adam's dream — he awoke and found it truth'. Adam had been dreaming about Eve.

Some time has been spent establishing the 'poetic' level at which desire operates. This can now be added to the original, more accessible levels of confession and theme. While the rest of the essay will attempt to use this three-tier system, inevitably the levels will dissolve into one another as we go deeper into the poems. The same will apply to the three main types of desire. The most immediate and fundamental category is the sexual one, to which can be added the spiritual and the aesthetic. The nature and importance of these areas will become apparent as we analyse them in turn.

A good deal has already been said about the centrality of eroticism in the poetry. Critics have pointed out how frequently sexual connotation abounds in the language, and how many objects and activities are sexually charged: drinking, eating, blushing, sleeping; fruit, the fragrance of flowers, and so on. The strength of the erotic impulse is registered in the fact that the original consummation scene in 'The Eve of St Agnes' was so explicit that Keats's publishers suppressed it. The revised version has to rely on strenuous imagery:

> Beyond a mortal man impassion'd far
> At these voluptuous accents, he arose,
> Ethereal, flush'd, and like a throbbing star
> Seen mid the sapphire heaven's deep repose
> Into her dream he melted, as the rose
> Blendeth its odour with the violet, —
> Solution sweet . . .

(ll.316–322)

Less remarked upon is the fact that this is a description of male gratification. The powerful phallic language of 'arose' and 'throbbing' is somewhat softened by the flower-fragrance image (the penetration), but the point of view is Porphyro's. As it must be, because Madeline is not yet awake. Although the poem is based on the lingering sexual expectations of both of them, Madeline's desire for the 'honey'd middle of the night' is quickly overshadowed by the 'purple riot' in Porphyro's heart. From the moment he enters the narrative his point of view dominates. We have no choice but to conspire or collaborate with his role as pleasure-seeker and voyeur. Madeline becomes an object of beauty to be literally ogled at. From his hidden position in her chamber, Porphyro is nothing less than a Peeping Tom. It may worry us to identify with a 'sexual fantasist' as one critic has called him. It is simply not the case that this poem is, like *Romeo and Juliet*, a tale of forbidden adolescent love. Porphyro is a sinister character. His 'stratagem' involves deceit and possibly ravishment. The description of Madeline undressing is a refined, caressing version of Hebe's unfortunate accident:

> . . . her vespers done,
> Of all its wreathed pearls her hair she frees;
> Unclasps her warmed jewels one by one;
> Loosens her fragrant boddice; by degrees
> Her rich attire creeps rustling to her knees

(ll.226–230)

The consummation is only partially what Madeline imagined it would be. In her trance-like supperless sleep she seems to be enjoying the company of a vision of Porphyro, but the real thing is another matter, provoking fear and alarm, desperation and disappointment. It is not clear whether she is properly awake. Porphyro melts into a dream in which she was being satisfied until he tried to wake her up. The word 'violet' may carry a suggestion of 'violate'. When Madeline genuinely wakes up she immediately accuses him of treachery. Porphyro has to draw on pseudo-religious romantic language to pacify her. There is nothing miraculous about his actions.

The myth on which 'The Eve of St Agnes' is based requires the expectant woman to become utterly passive; to assume a death-like, statuesque supineness. Female sexual desire is not allowed to be assertive. Or, if it is, it is traditionally dangerous, treacherous and threatening to men. This is the case in 'Endymion', 'Lamia' and 'La Belle Dame sans Merci'. Female desire is a denial of the male prerogative.

There are no images of equal, reciprocal, healthy sexual desire in the poems. This applies to the orgiastic scenes depicted on the Grecian urn. The pagan males are in 'mad pursuit' of 'maidens loth', a reluctant if tantalising quarry. If there is any 'wild ecstasy', it is strictly for the male hunter-lover:

> Bold Lover, never, never canst thou kiss,
> Though winning near the goal — yet, do not grieve;
> She cannot fade, though thou hast not thy bliss,
> For ever wilt thou love, and she be fair!
>
> (ll.17–20)

The denial is of course a trick of representational art. The 'cold' marble freezes but animates a passionate action. It requires some elasticity of logic however to see this never-ending male desire as 'happy'. As the temperature rises the physical cost becomes apparent:

> More happy love! more happy, happy love!
> For ever warm and still to be enjoy'd,
> For ever panting, and for ever young;
> All breathing human passion far above,
> That leaves a heart high-sorrowful and cloy'd,
> A burning forehead, and a parching tongue.
>
> (ll.25–30)

There seem to be more losses than gains, The grim consequences of permanent lust rest uneasily with the ethereal 'passion far above'.

The confessional and poetic levels of sexual desire coalesce most strikingly in 'Ode to Psyche'. The desire to be a great poet is presented in erotic mythological terms. Psyche represents beauty. She has been a neglected deity. Keats wishes to remedy this oversight. He will be her modern priest, celebrating her virtues in his verse. This role requires the ousting of her traditional lover Cupid, who is not mentioned after the first stanza. Instead it is the poet who desires to 'make a moan/ Upon the midnight hours' (ll.44–45) as he builds a temple for Psyche inside his mind. Allegorically this 'fane' is Keats's future output and his immortality. Inside this 'rosy sanctuary' built with the help of fancy there will be a regular nocturnal meeting with beauty. The process if not the outcome will be 'all soft delight/ That shadowy thought can win' (ll.64–65). The closing detail of the 'casement ope at night,/ To let the warm Love in' is strongly suggestive of the sexual act. Psyche is therefore a relative of the mind-mistresses of 'Fancy' and of the muse of poetry who was believed traditionally to visit the male poet in his sleep and inspire him. Keats's 'working brain' is sexually and poetically active. In a letter of October 1818 already quoted, he refers to his composition as 'my night's labours'. His amoral and mischievous 'camelion' poetic identity is also described as continually 'filling some other Body'. One receptacle might be the 'unravish'd', womb-like Grecian urn.

The next category to consider is spiritual desire. The needs of the soul might seem to be diametrically opposed to those of the flesh. Carnal desire is selfish, immediate, transient, changeable, unreliable, destructive, mortal. Spiritual desire is self-liberating, permanent, pure, transcendent, healing, sublime, immortal. The satisfaction of the spirit can be a compensation for the imperfections of the material world. This polarity can be seen in much religious and philosophical thought. On closer inspection, however, the two needs are seen to be related, particularly as the immaterial can only be described in material terms. The word 'ecstasy', for instance, has a secular and religious meaning. The 'wild ecstasy' depicted on the Grecian urn is no doubt a release of physical and religious energy in a fertility ritual. So the gratification of the spirit need not mean suppression of one's sexuality. The two can be complementary, or in permanent power-struggle. When Keats devised a theory of salvation to rival the Christian belief in this world as a 'vale of tears' he drew on a fleshly image to clinch his point: 'a World of Pains and troubles is . . . the teat from which the Mind or intelligence sucks its identity' (letter to George and Georgiana Keats, 21 April 1819).

This remark takes us straight to one of Keats's best poems about the desire for immortality: the sonnet 'Bright Star'. The poet wants to be 'steadfast' or constant. He looks to a traditional image of this (the star) but finds its qualities lacking in certain key respects. The poet wants 'unchangeable' love and affection. The comparison with the star is therefore superseded by a more perfect image of the poet 'pillow'd' on his lover's 'ripening breast' in 'sweet unrest'. The star's 'splendour' is protective and watchful, but also distant, cold, and lonely. The star is compared to a 'sleepless Eremite' or hermit, a religious recluse devoted to ascetic spiritual insomnia and self-denial, secretive and abstracted. The poet prefers 'unchangeable' physical intimacy which combines sexual arousal (the lover's breast is 'ripening'), a healing and protective natural rhythm (the 'fall and swell' of her 'tender-taken breath' replaces the more distant sea and snow scenes of lines 5–8) and an ultimate, ambiguous oblivion — 'swoon to death' conveys carnal and spiritual satisfaction. The poet's ideal 'fair love' is not a goddess. The ethereal realm of the heavens is rejected. The 'sweet unrest' of a lover's embrace is a more human ideal of permanence than the sterile sleeplessness of the bright star. 'I am certain of nothing but of the holiness of the Heart's affections' said Keats (letter to Bailey, 22 November 1817). The lovers in the sonnet are as holy as the 'priestlike' stars. Salvation lies in our own grasp.

'Bright Star' is yet another nocturnal encounter between the poet and an ideal experience. Any attempt to transcend the 'World of Pains and troubles' is rejected in favour of a conquest from within. These two solutions to life's problems are explored more elaborately in Keats's most famous confessional poem 'Ode to a Nightingale'. The poet wishes to swallow a 'draught of vintage' and 'fade away' into the nightingale's 'embalmed' darkness; to pass beyond the 'leaden-eyed despairs' of consciousness into a rich mystical oblivion, a superior form of dissolution on a plane with the bird's invisible 'ecstacy'. The ode has been seen as a death-wish haunted by the recent death of Keats's brother Tom and foreshadowing the poet's own fatal illness. Such a view is simplistic and does not take account of the complex role of the 'viewless wings of Poesy'. The desired 'draught of vintage' has poetical properties — it is 'Full of the true, the blushful Hippocrene' (which is a spring sacred to the muses) — but only the power of poetry can cross the threshold of the 'dull brain'. The amount of satisfaction the poet experiences in the four-stanza journey to and from the nightingale is considerable, and must not be minimised as a mere failure of the imagination. The desire to 'fade away' is granted. The poet is liberated from 'The weariness, the fever, and the fret' of the mortal world in so far as they press upon his discarded consciousness. The 'embalmed darkness' and passive state of the poet resemble death (a distant echo of the sleeping Madeline). Given this dissolution it is not surprising the poet should confess to being 'half in love with easeful Death' as Death is a kind of permanent swooning, a pleasurable loss of perceptions. The 'happy lot' of the bird's beautiful song is now an 'ecstasy' of immortal passion. Only the wings of poetry have permitted access to this revelation. Moreover the importance of suffering is not entirely forgotten. It re-enters with the portrait of Ruth. The journey she desires back to her home is in the opposite direction to the poet's. She longs to escape or be released from her exile in 'alien corn'. The poet has escaped from his home (consciousness) into an 'alien' darkness. But the inability to sustain this liberation is another important insight yielded by 'Poesy'. Ruth's suffering recalls the necessary suffering of the path to salvation, and therefore Ruth's desired journey anticipates the poet's return to his 'sole self'. As Keats said in his 'vale of Soul-making' theory, 'how necessary a World of Pains and troubles is to school an Intelligence and make it a soul' (letter to George and Georgiana Keats, 21 April 1819). The final insight is that the ability of poetry to provide spiritual gratification is limited: 'the fancy cannot cheat so well/ As she is fam'd to do, deceiving elf'. Desire and its denial fertilise each other, as Ruth's tears nourish the corn she must work in. The poet is left in that characteristic, productive half-slumber — 'Do

I wake or sleep?' — awaiting the next nightly labour.

Our final category of aesthetic desire includes the impulse to touch, possess or create beauty, as well as the desire for fame and success as a poet. Some of the remarks in his letters have led to Keats acquiring a reputation as a worshipper of beauty, the priest at Psyche's temple. In the poems we find famous statements such as 'A thing of beauty is a joy for ever' (the opening of 'Endymion') and 'Beauty is truth, truth beauty' (the ending of 'Ode on a Grecian Urn'). These dictums must not be applied to Keats's poems like labels, nor as short-cuts to interpretation. The conclusion to 'Ode on a Grecian Urn' is notoriously unreliable, having nothing or everything to do with the rest of the poem. The celebration of beauty in art and life is a complex issue in the poems, as we have now come to expect. Our discussion will focus on the two odes that have not yet received attention, 'Indolence' and 'Melancholy'.

'Ode to Psyche' brought together the poet's sexual and poetical ambitions. In 'Ode on Indolence', however, the different strands of Love, Ambition and Poesy are separated into distinct allegorical presences who visit the poet in a waking dream. They are not all equally appealing. Love is a 'fair Maid'. Ambition is genderless and sickly. Poesy is also female and produces the strongest reaction because the poet loves her. Poesy is like a *femme fatale*: 'unmeek' (assertive) and a 'demon' (an influence he cannot do without). The three figures appear to tempt the poet, and he aches with the desire to follow them as they begin to fade. Allegorically this means the most important things in the poet's life are being denied him, dangled tantalisingly before him yet beyond his reach as he does not yet have 'wings' of poetic power he will use in 'Ode to a Nightingale'. But his ache soon changes to stern defiance. The desire for 'wings' is rejected in the third stanza as a 'folly' because the quest for all three goals would be a vain one, a dead end. The poet takes a cynical position. Love does not exist. Ambition (success in bettering oneself socially) is a 'short fever-fit' of our 'little heart' (and in any case it had a 'fatigued eye' through constant striving) — hardly a pleasurable experience. As for Poesy, the pleasures she can bring are nothing at the side of the self-reliant gratification of the half-slumber of 'honied indolence'. There is no need to aspire to be a great poet courting public acclaim ('A pet-lamb in a sentimental farce'). Indolence will provide 'visions for the night'. This reminds us of the armchair fantasies in 'Fancy'. The poet turns inward, not allowing his 'Phantom' visitors to hurt him.

So in the 'Ode on Indolence' the quest for beauty is defiantly rejected. In 'Ode on Melancholy', on the other hand, we do penetrate Beauty's 'very temple of Delight' and the sexual and poetical are once again firmly intertwined. The ode is not written in the confessional mode but in an odd combination of second person (stanzas 1 and 2) and third person (stanza 3). The generic 'you' is advised how best to use a 'melancholy fit'. The first stanza dismisses any attempt to draw on magical or mythical rituals in order to seek oblivion. The best way to satisfy the 'wakeful anguish of the soul' is outlined in the second stanza. Rather than try to escape sensation, one should 'glut' oneself with the pleasurable experiences of this world. To 'glut' is to indulge to excess, to over-fill. Such a surfeit of sensuous pleasure can be supplied by the beauty of nature (morning rose, rainbow, 'wealth of globed peonies') or the inevitable 'mistress'. The latter option is described in a disturbing fashion:

> Or if thy mistress some rich anger shows,
>   Emprison her soft hand, and let her rave,
>   And feed deep, deep upon her peerless eyes.

The repetition of 'deep, deep' feeding achieves a continuity with the idea of a 'glut' on a 'rich' experience, but the pleasure is clearly sadistic. The eroticism is distasteful and seems unnecessary and incongruous. To understand if not excuse its presence we have to look at the final stanza. There we see that the cruel conjunction of pain and pleasure is the general, melancholic order of things:

> She dwells with Beauty — Beauty that must die;
>   And Joy, whose hand is ever at his lips
> Bidding adieu; and aching Pleasure nigh,
>   Turning to poison while the bee-mouth sips

This is a philosophically pessimistic insight, the culmination of the generalisations we found in 'Fancy'. The climax of this bittersweet condition is Melancholy's 'temple of Delight'. This is reminiscent of Psyche's temple but this time the poetical—sexual element is strongly laced with obliteration. The male poet enters this 'sovran shrine' at his peril. The power relations between the sexes that applied in the outside world and enabled him to 'emprison' his mistress's hand are reversed. Though he has an élite 'strenuous tongue' of hedonistic experience (quaffing drink, with added associations of speaking (poetry) and oral sexual activity) which qualifies him to have access, the cost of enjoying a 'taste' of Melancholy's beauty is death. He will be 'among her cloudy trophies hung'. This reminds us of the male sexual paranoia of 'La Belle Dame sans Merci' and more locally of the fate of the male bee that mates with the Queen. To find beauty is a great and terrible achievement. The 'glut' has proved fatal. Once the poet has penetrated the temple of Delight, there is no going further. There are no desires left. The supreme gratification has been granted. The 'cloudy trophy' is a symbol of success and loss. The trophy is 'cloudy' — in an ethereal region above this world, but also indistinct, uncertain. As a trophy it is a sign of victory, but also of death and defeat. It is a perfect symbol of the complex issues this essay has been investigating.

AFTERTHOUGHTS

1

Explain the sense in which Haywood is using 'desire' in this essay.

2

Should a feminist disapprove of Keats's poetry?

3

What relationship is there in Keats's poetry between death and desire?

4

Why does Haywood describe the 'cloudy trophy' in the 'Ode on Melancholy' as 'a perfect symbol of the complex issues this essay has been investigating'?

Joy Flint

Joy Flint has many years' experience as a teacher and Senior Examiner, and has edited Silas Marner *for Longman Study Texts.*

ESSAY

Keats's letters and poetry: a life of sensations

'Here are the poems — they will explain themselves — as all poems should do without comment.' Keats was writing to his brother George in January 1819, enclosing copies of his most recent work. He had expressed similar views on the self-sufficiency of poetry to his publisher John Taylor in February 1818: 'Its touches of Beauty should never be half way ther[e] by making the reader breathless instead of content: the rise, the progress, the setting of the imagery should like the Sun come natural too him'. He might have been describing the progress through the, as yet unwritten, ode 'To Autumn'.

All Keats's most familiar poetry, whether directly descriptive or, in its medieval or classical setting, remotely narrative, has this quality of natural completeness. The 'plaintive anthem fades', 'the sedge has wither'd from the lake', the lovers flee away into the storm. Many readers of Keats share his reluctance to comment on the finished poems: the natural kind of poetry he sought to write inhibits intrusive examination. Words unfold unobtrusively into the precise sensation he wishes to recreate: the poetry comes 'as naturally as the leaves to a tree'.

The fluency of Keats's verse and, to some modern readers, the easy attractiveness of his subject-matter, can suggest that his poetry lacks experience and thought, that it comes too 'naturally'. His letters undeceive us.

Reading them — mis-spelt, half-punctuated — as they flow spontaneously through trivial gossip, literary allusion, nonsense, half-formulated ideas, and the record of personal pain and distress, we are in intimate contact with a mind wholly absorbed with poetry. 'The Genius of Poetry must work out its own salvation in a man', he wrote to Hessey in October 1818, speaking of the imperfections and immaturities of 'Endymion' and stressing the value of learning through the practice of his craft — 'It cannot be matured by law and precept, but by sensation and watchfulness in itself'. The letters give us both a generous self-revelation of the man and a poet's notebook — more human and immediate, less clinical and pedantic than those of his successor Gerard Manley Hopkins.

We can read the poems themselves with the benefit of his own comments on the nature of poetry and of the poet, on the progress of his own maturing imagination and technical skill. The letters emphasise for us the extent to which poetry was an integral part of Keats's life and the depth to which it was felt and lived. Poetry was never set apart: it was the medium through which he lived more intensely. 'I find I cannot exist without poetry . . . half the day will not do . . .', he wrote to Reynolds in April 1817; and to Bailey in August 1819: 'I am convinced more and more every day that a fine writer is the most genuine Being in the world'. 'This state of excitement in me . . .', he wrote, again to Reynolds, in August 1819, 'it is the only state for the best sort of Poetry — that is all I care for, all I live for.'

The sensation of living and the experience of poetry were inseparable for Keats. When he attempts to express what he feels about the nature of poetry, even in the earliest tentative speculations in 'I stood tip-toe upon a little hill' he does so through analogy with other forms of experience. The 'dear delight/ Of this fair world' (ll.116–117) is what makes a poet, and poetry is defined in nature's terms:

> In the calm grandeur of a sober line,
> We see the waving of the mountain pine

(ll.127–128)

When he writes of the 'old poets' he speaks of 'Miltonian storms' and of 'Spenserian vowels that elope with ease,/ And float along like birds o'er summer seas'.

To Keats the urbane poets of the eighteenth century were stale, mere 'handicraftsmen', without feeling for the forms of nature:

> The winds of heaven blew, the ocean roll'd
> Its gathering waves — ye felt it not.
>   . . . the dew
> Of summer nights collected still to make
> The morning precious: beauty was awake!
> Why were ye not awake?
>
>   ('Sleep and Poetry', ll.188–193)

The subject-matter of his own poems may appear conventional to modern readers but the poets of his generation had rediscovered the natural source of poetry, the natural world. It was intoxicating to Keats; it had to be felt and experienced. He speaks of poetry as a living, growing thing; as he writes in his sonnet to Spenser:

> The flower must drink the nature of the soil
>   Before it can put forth its blossoming

The line of his verse must reflect and re-create each intensified experience.

His early poetry overflows with too lush an abundance of sensation. He watches over each sense experience, as Hopkins was to do later, until the words and phrases chosen convey exactly the qualities of the thing described, or reflect patterns of sight and sound and movement. A pigeon is 'tumbling in clear summer air', a swan with 'neck of arch'd snow' 'oared himself along with majesty', 'The willow trails/ Its delicate amber':

> . . . swarms of minnows show their little heads
> Staying their wavy bodies 'gainst the streams,
> To taste the luxury of sunny beams
> Temper'd with coolness. . . .
> If you but scantily hold our your hand,
> That very instant not one will remain;
> But turn your eye, and they are there again.
>
>   ('I stood tip-toe upon a little hill', ll.72–80)

In his earliest poetry he was consciously living the 'Life of Sensations rather than of Thoughts' of which he wrote in a letter to Bailey in November 1817. A poet watches the world as keenly as any naturalist:

> To his sight
> The husk of natural objects opens quite
> To the core; and every secret essence there
> Reveals the elements of good and fair
>
> ('The Poet', ll.4–7)

Keats is learning his craft 'by sensation and watchfulness in itself'. He is feeling his way by prodigal and adventurous experiment:

> . . . scarce knowing my intent;
> Still scooping up the water with my fingers,
> In which a trembling diamond never lingers.
>
> ('To Charles Cowden Clarke', ll.18–20)

In his attempt to re-create living sensations in words, he feels his way simultaneously towards a greater understanding of the world and of the nature of poetry.

Keats learned to curb his early exuberance, to become a 'miser of sound and syllable' so that he could contain, within a single word or line — 'globed peonies' or 'quick pattereth the flaw-blown sleet' or 'mild as a star in water' or 'the tiger-moth's deep-damask'd wings' — a faithful sense impression to be released on reading.

The poet watching the minnows is still able to 'scantily hold out the hand' to make them move. He does not yet share their existence as he does that of the sparrow which comes before his window: 'I take part in its existince and pick about the Gravel'. He was to become imaginatively absorbed into the unique nature of everything he observed. The early Keats in 'Endymion' finds the exact word to describe the sound of the 'wailful gnat'; he is not yet so fully absorbed in its life that his verse moves naturally into the rhythm of its wider existence:

> Then in a wailful choir the small gnats mourn
> Among the river sallows, borne aloft
> Or sinking as the light wind lives or dies
>
> ('To Autumn', ll.27–29)

Patient observation has deepened into a full consciousness of the living creature. In a letter to Woodhouse in October 1818 Keats speaks of the 'camelion Poet' — the kind of poet he believed himself to be — whose nature changes with his subject, and says of him that he has no personal identity, he is continually 'filling some other Body — The Sun, the Moon, the Sea and Men and Women who are creatures of impulse are poetical and have about them an unchangeable attribute — the poet has none; no identity'.

The growth of an individual, feeling consciousness is a recurrent theme in Keats's poems, early and late. The dreaming Endymion senses a dimension that exists beyond his daylight world and for which he searches all his waking hours. The young Apollo in 'Hyperion' is visited by dreams and in 'aching ignorance' craves knowledge from the goddess. The search for understanding is coupled with a growing awareness of the latent power of poetry — in the reworked version, 'The Fall of Hyperion', it is, explicitly, the Poet who seeks enlightenment, who aches:

> To see as a god sees, and take the depth
> Of things as nimbly as the outward eye
> Can size and shape pervade.

(ll.304–306)

As Keats's own knowledge widens and deepens the enchanted dreams of 'Endymion' give way to the darker visions he describes in his verse letter to Reynolds in March 1818:

> Still do I that most fierce destruction see, —
> The Shark at savage prey, — the Hawk at pounce, —
> The gentle Robin, like a Pard or Ounce,
> Ravening a worm

(ll.102–105)

Writing to him again in May, he asserts that 'an extensive knowledge is needful to thinking people' and compares 'human life to a large Mansion of Many Apartments' through which we move from a 'thoughtless' chamber to one in which thinking is awakened and our vision 'into the heart and nature of Man' is sharpened to an awareness of suffering. He finds himself in this room and the many doors that open from it, and which he must explore, are dark.

His letters in the later part of this year are full of his consciousness of his dying younger brother: 'His identity presses upon me so all day that I am obliged to go out ... I am obliged to write, and plunge into abstract images to ease myself of his countenance his voice his feebleness'.

Keats's poetry was always aware of mortality. In 'Sleep and Poetry' he knows:

> ... life is but a day;
> A fragile dew-drop on its perilous way
> From a tree's summit

(ll.85–87)

and that the time when he can 'sleep in the grass' and 'Feed on apples red, and strawberries', will given way to 'a nobler life' where he 'may find the agonies, the strife/ Of human hearts'. In this poem he examines the nature of poetry and sees clearly that to dwell too long on the 'burrs,/ And thorns of life' is to distort the truth. The Gothic — 'trees uptorn/ Darkness, and worms, and shrouds, and sepulchres', as we know from 'Isabella' and from 'La Belle Dame sans Merci', had its attractions for Keats, as it had for his contemporaries. After the fashion of Leigh Hunt,[1] he knew it to be as unhealthy for the imagination as an over-indulgence in sweets. Keats conceived the function of poetry and the role of the poet in the terms of the calling to which he was first apprenticed: medicine. He sees the poet as healer, poetry as health-giving. The great end of poetry, he says in 'Sleep and Poetry' — anticipating the 'Ode on a Grecian Urn' — is to be:

> ... a friend
> To sooth the cares and lift the thoughts of man.

(ll.246–247)

In 'The Fall of Hyperion' Keats still uses these terms:

> ... sure a poet is a sage;
> A humanist, Physician to all men.

(ll.189–190)

---

[1] Leight Hunt, 1784–1859, essayist and poet. Keats's first published poem appeared in Hunt's journal, *The Examiner*, and his very early work was influenced by Hunt's style.

The poet is in and of this world; 'nothing ever becomes real till it is experienced' — Fancy proves 'a deceiving elf':

> The poet and the dreamer are distinct,
> Diverse, sheer opposite, antipodes.
> The one pours out a balm upon the world,
> The other vexes it.

(ll.199–202)

Keats's early poetry dwells on and seeks words to convey his own delight in the sensations of the world around him. Increasingly his response is permeated by his sharpened human consciousness. He is less and less a detached observer, even of nature; in May 1818, he tells Reynolds: 'I lay awake last night listening to the Rain with a sense of being drown'd and rotted like a grain of wheat'. Increasingly he experiences a world that is both 'sweet and bitter'; increasingly he comes to understand 'how necessary a World of Pains and troubles is to school an intelligence and make it a Soul' that 'the heart must feel and suffer in a thousand diverse ways'.

Consciousness of the precariousness of life, of the vulnerability of joy, intensifies his experience of its richness and beauty. He tries in his poetry to see the balance of good and evil, to understand and reconcile life's contraries. In 'The Eve of St Agnes' the climax of youthful passion is more intensely realised as it is poised in its moment of full summer within the threatening winter storm and the proximity of the dying and the dead. Even at the very moment when Porphyro kneels by the side of Madeline he is 'pale as smooth-sculptured stone'.

'These lovers fled away into the storm': the moment of enchantment passes. But it lingers and is not destroyed. It prompts old Angela 'weak in body and in soul' to conspire with Porphyro; and though 'the joys of all his life were said and sung' the patient, holy Beadsman can be 'flatter'd to tears' by 'Music's golden tongue'.

As early as 'Endymion' Keats recognised that:

> There never liv'd a mortal man, who bent
> His appetite beyond his natural sphere
> But starv'd and died.

(Book IV, ll.646–648)

The will to experience passion outside and beyond his natural sphere leaves the Knight-at-arms 'Alone and palely loitering' and Lycius's arms 'empty of delight'. For all the 'warm cloister'd hours' spent there, Lamia's palace remains a cheat and a delusion, her consuming, self-willed, self-absorbed passion, destructive and terror-laden. By contrast the tender unfolding love of Isabella and Lorenzo, though so violently ended, is unblighted and leaves behind a lingering fragrance:

> The little sweet doth kill much bitterness
>
> (stanza XIII)

Keats's belief in the integrity of the living moment convinces him that 'too many tears for lovers have been shed'. It does not diminish his capacity to suffer with them. Isabella's sorrow is conveyed simply and directly but the dead Lorenzo yearns for the sensations and sounds of life with a deeper anguish:

> . . . those sounds grow strange to me,
> And thou art distant in Humanity.
>
> I know what was, I feel full well what is
>
> (stanzas XXXIX–XL)

As his letters show, his brother's death and his own increasingly feverish health strengthen Keats's fears that he may 'cease to be' — that Humanity will grow distant to him, that he will lose the power to feel and experience, to know joy and sorrow. The gap between the living and the dead widens. He tries to imagine the impossible, 'the feel of not to feel it' ('Stanzas: In a drear-nighted December'). The branches of winter trees may not remember 'Their green felicity' but the feeling human being must, like Lorenzo, stretch out towards life. In a strange fragment of verse Keats imagines the inconceivable moment 'When this warm scribe my hand is in the grave':

> This living hand, now warm and capable
> Of earnest grasping, would, if it were cold
> And in the icy silence of the tomb,
> So haunt thy days and chill thy dreaming nights
> That thou wouldst wish thine own heart dry of blood
> So in my veins red life might stream again

There were other times when his consciousness of distress and pain could make the prospect of death and oblivion seductive:

> Now more than ever seems it rich to die,
> > To cease upon the midnight with no pain
>
> > > ('Ode to a Nightingale', ll.55–56)

Yet he remains only 'half in love with easeful Death'. To have 'ears in vain', no longer to hear the nightingale, to become — in all the deaf finality of its monosyllable — 'a sod', a piece of earth, is inconceivable.

Yet the tension between life and death, between joy and sorrow, was necessary to Keats. His perception of it made him a poet. Even in the last of his letters in November 1820, leading what he feels to be 'a posthumous existence', his mind is still occupied with the nature of poetry and its relationship to experience. He writes to Charles Brown: 'the knowledge of contrast, feeling for light and shade' is the 'primitive sense' necessary for a poem.

We find Keats's most concentrated and mature handling of the contrasts and tensions which he perceived in life, in the odes published in the 1820 volume. They draw together all the concerns that have occupied his mind — both as a man and as a poet — in his letters and in his poetry. His own distinctive voice had long been heard in his poetry; in the odes he discovered his own form.

Mastering the forms used by 'the old poets', in his long apprenticeship to them, taught him to curb the natural profusion of his early style. His devotion to Shakespeare's sonnets and his own practice of the form taught him the value of isolating a single thought or feeling. Simple narrative, as in 'The Eve of St Agnes', encouraged him to concentrate on a single emotion. The strictly disciplined fourteen lines of the sonnet, however, were narrow and restrictive; he needed greater scope:

> Let us find out, if we must be constrain'd,
> > Sandals more interwoven and complete
> To fit the naked foot of Poesy
>
> > > ('On the Sonnet', ll.4–6)

The sonnet-related stanza forms Keats used in the odes combine the restraint of the sonnet with greater freedom to explore the intricate web of sensations, images and thoughts prompted by a single subject. He is able to hold his subject in focus and let it develop its natural length, its natural structure: the duration of a nightingale's song, the course of an autumn day, or the turning of a Grecian urn in the hand.

Keats died before the 'genius of poetry' had fully 'worked out its own salvation' in him. Looking at the odes, at four of them in particular — 'on Melancholy'; 'on a Grecian Urn'; 'to a Nightingale'; 'To Autumn' — it is tempting to see an unconscious, tentative movement, not towards dramatic form, where his inclination and aspirations lay, but towards a complex musical structure like the one T S Eliot was to develop more deliberately and intellectually when attempting in the *Four Quartets* to explore and resolve some of the same paradoxes which had perplexed Keats in an earlier generation.

Taken together the four odes achieve a meditative unity. Each has its own distinctive character, yet each sheds light on the experience of others; each at some point touches on the images, the sensations, the emotions, the perceptions of the others. Each is conscious of the cycle of the moving year and fleetingly recalls the inverse season: the 'happy melodist' of spring beneath the trees that cannot shed their leaves is recalled in Autumn; the 'embalmed darkness' of the summer nightingale, no less than the 'ruby grape of Proserpine' moves Lethe-wards.

Each of the four odes isolates and explores a single experience. 'Each venture', in Eliot's words in 'East Coker', 'Is a new beginning, a raid on the inarticulate', each ode a new approach through poetry to the perplexities that 'tease us out of thought'. Keats approaches the mysteries of the relationship of pleasure to pain, of art to life, of the conflict between man's perception of the eternal and of his mortal nature — as he has always done — through sensations rather than through thoughts. He does so with an intensity of realisation that has the force of thought.

In the 'Ode on Melancholy' Keats explores the proximity of pleasure to pain. The message is the same as in his letters: 'Do you not see how necessary a World of Pains and troubles is to school an Intelligence and make it a Soul?' (to George and Georgiana Keats, April 1819). Descent to Lethe — to lose the sensations of the living world — is inconceivable, beauty is felt more keenly in the knowledge that it must die; 'the wakeful anguish of the soul' is necessary to the full perception of happiness. Momentarily, caught in the equivocal sound, the two contrary sensations touch in the image of 'a morning rose'.

In the 'Ode on a Grecian Urn' the verbal ambiguities suggest the teasing perplexities that arise when he considers the urn and the relationship of art to life. His view of the role of art is expressed in the terms he used in 'Sleep and Poetry': its function is consolatory, to be 'a friend to man', to bring the timeless and healing knowledge that the perception of truth involves beauty and the perception of beauty involves the recognition of truth. Art can suspend movement, stay the seasons, create eternal spring and delight 'still to be enjoy'd' but its figures remain silent, remain 'still', far removed from 'breathing human passion'; the sacrifice that life entails remains unmade. The 'Ode on a Grecian Urn' appeals to the eye and to the mind. Keats re-creates its visual impact with remarkable clarity, his other senses unengaged. The urn remains a marble shape: the imagery is drained of colour, the melodies unheard. Only the sacrificial heifer led to the altar — 'all her silken flanks with garlands drest' — can we reach out and touch.

Keats was never more absorbed in sensation than when reliving his experience of the nightingale's song, his senses never more fully engaged. He is 'too happy' in its summer happiness, deliberately holding the living experience in mortal hands. Consciousness that 'youth grows pale, and spectre-thin, and dies' sharpens his full awareness of the experience until, momentarily, he can perceive, in Eliot's 'Little Gidding' phrase, 'the intersection of the timeless moment' through the bird's song.

The three stanzas of the ode 'To Autumn' are Keats's most complete realisation of his idea, expressed in a letter to Reynolds in February 1818, that poetry should be 'unobtrusive, a thing which enters into one's soul, and does not startle it or amaze it with itself, but with its subject', that it should come 'as naturally as the Leaves to a tree'. The poet's presence in the ode is unobtrusive but the concentration of sense impressions has never been more exact and more entire; the diction and cadences have never reflected more nearly the living experience. Active verbs and participles move the poem imperceptibly as time through an autumn day. As mists give way to drowsy noon and hours fade into the 'soft-dying day', the wider movement of the year is felt; summer passes into autumn and, tinged with regret for spring, dies into winter. At the heart of the ode, Autumn is personified as the harvester: here 'the next swath' is only for an instant spared by art. The corn is not alien; the living human figure is integral to the landscape.

AFTERTHOUGHTS

1

Do you agree with Keats that all poems should 'explain themselves ... without comment' (opening paragraph)?

2

What development does this essay trace in Keats's work?

3

Do you agree that Keats 'always' approaches his subject 'through sensations rather than through thoughts' (page 87)?

4

Have the letters helped or hindered your appreciation of the poems?

Graham Holderness

Graham Holderness is Head of the Drama Department at the Roehampton Institute of Higher Education, and has published numerous books and critical articles.

ESSAY

Sensuous language in Keats's odes

> O for a Life of Sensations rather than of Thoughts!
>
> > (Keats, letter to Bailey, 22 November 1817)

The poetry of Keats has always been recognised as displaying a characteristically 'sensuous' use of language. The term can mean a number of different things, and critical attitudes towards 'sensuousness' in poetry vary greatly.

We usually understand the description to refer initially to certain poetic qualities; and then, by implication, to a certain approach to life or experience which those qualities may be thought to entail. A 'sensuous' poetry is one intensively concerned (as perhaps all poetry is to *some* degree concerned) to activate and appeal to our senses of sight, hearing, smell, taste and touch. Keats's poetry obviously works by encouraging us to perceive — to *feel* — vivid and distinct sensuous impressions.

> I cannot see what flowers are at my feet,
> > Nor what soft incense hangs upon the boughs

Stanza 5 of the 'Ode to a Nightingale' alludes to the sense of sight, or its absence ('I cannot see'); the senses of touch and of smell ('soft incense'); and by the end of the verse, with its evocation of 'the coming musk-rose, full of dewy wine,/ The murmurous haunt of flies', the senses of taste and hearing have also been incorporated.

A general recognition of this quality leads to the concensus that Keats's poetry is particularly successful at depicting, representing or conveying 'reality' or 'experience': that his poetic language displays a kind of 'solidity' or 'concreteness' capable of convincing the reader of the reality of what it communicates — persuading you, almost, to imagine that you are literally perceiving the objects and the experiences that the verse describes. The most influential critical account of this view can be found in an essay by F R Leavis, published in his book *Revaluation* (London, 1936). Leavis starts with Keats's strongly realised sensuous impressions, quoting a phrase from the 'Ode on Melancholy' — 'the wealth of globed peonies'.

> . . . the hand is round the peony, luxuriously cupping it. Such tactual effects are notoriously characteristic of Keats, and they express, not merely the voluptuary's itch to be fingering, but that strong grasp upon actualities — upon things outside himself, that firm sense of the solid world, that makes Keats so different from Shelley.
>
> (pp.261–262)

This initial suggestion is not that the poet was holding a peony while writing the poem, or that the reader miraculously finds himself holding one: but that the poem's sensuous language imaginatively convinces you, the reader, as you read the line, that *this must be what it would feel like if you were literally holding, at the moment, a flower in your hand.* Discussing the same line in another context Leavis commented:

> This palpability of 'globèd' — the word doesn't merely describe, or refer to, the sensation, but gives a tactual image. It is as if one were actually cupping the peony with one's hand. So elsewhere, in reading poetry, one responds as if one were making a given kind of movement or a given kind of effort . . . In reading a successful poem it is as if . . . one were living that particular action, situation or piece of life.
>
> ('Imagery and Movement', *Scrutiny* XIII, *1945*)

That kind of 'tactual image' instances the poet's 'strong grasp upon actualities', his 'firm sense of the solid world'; with the result that we are convinced of the objective reality of the experiences the poems convey, and the truth of the imaginative world they describe.

These sensuous details, which can easily be located and analysed in the poetry, have frequently been regarded as expressive or symptomatic of certain characteristics of the author's personality or philosophy of life. Thus hostile criticism of Keats's poetry has often implied that sensuousness in poetry is a kind of vice or moral weakness, self-evidently inferior to intellectual abstraction, moral wisdom and spiritual enlightenment. Favourable criticism defends the sensuous as a legitimate poetic medium, directing the poetic imagination towards its proper activity, the pursuit of beauty and truth. Some of the phrases used by Leavis in the passage just quoted, in their harsh moral contempt for mere sensuousness — 'notoriously characteristic', 'the voluptuary's itch to be fingering' — indicate that this particular critic could never value sensuousness in poetry unless it was accompanied by intelligence and moral curiosity. For Leavis, Keats's strength as a poet is not so much that he conveys vivid images of sensuous experience, as that his sensuous qualities can persuade us he possessed a firm grasp of objective reality.

Like all literary criticism, Leavis's was based in a particular philosophy of language. Underlying his comments on Keats's poetry are certain presuppositions about poetry in general: that its language can depict or represent the reality of experience; that it should not rest content merely to aim at vivid sensuous effects, but should employ intelligence, wit and moral sensitivity to organise the sensuous impressions into a coherent intellectual structure; and that this combination of feeling and thought is the most perfect vehicle for realising and conveying reality and truth. In itself this theory of language gives rise to problems and contradictions; and developments in linguistics over the last twenty years or so have made Leavis's assumptions about the nature of poetic language highly questionable.

To start with, if a poem conveys both sensuous experience and intellectual truth, thought and feeling, 'emotions' and 'ideas', then it must be entering into a different relationship with reality in each case. If a poem conveys feeling via its appeal to the senses, then, we assume, it is conveying some common or even universal human experience which we can recognise and identify with. When the poet or narrator of 'Ode to a Nightingale' says:

>   . . . for many a time
> I have been half in love with easeful Death

(ll.51–52)

he seems to be presenting a personal experience for general recognition: this has happened to him 'many a time', this is how it felt, and we the readers can, if not recognise, at least appreciate what it must feel like to regard death as an 'easeful' release from care and suffering. We don't necessarily assume that Keats is telling us, or seeking to persuade us, that this death-wish is a good thing, or a valuable experience, or an impulse to be celebrated. We simply acknowledge it as one feeling among others that the poem is communicating: and some of those other feelings may well contradict the love of death:

> Still wouldst thou sing, and I have ears in vain —
>   To thy high requiem become a sod.

(ll.59–60)

The erotic desire for, and the sensuous 'love' of death, could lead the poet to an extinction of the senses: to become a mere piece of earth, dead to all sensation, impervious to the beauty of the nightingale's song.

But if on the other hand the poem is communicating an idea — an attitude, a philosophical proposition, a moral view — then we are much more likely to recognise it as something personal to the poet, a view he may have held and regarded as true, and of the truth of which he wished to convince his readers. This is no longer a matter of experience (which, it is assumed, we all have in common) but a matter of ideas which we know differ from person to person, social group to social group, age to age. 'Experience' is assumed to be a basic core of human reality, while 'ideas' are questionable propositions relative to individual, social and historical circumstances. The famous lines which close the 'Ode on a Grecian Urn' have often been received as a statement of Keats's personal philosophy:

Beauty is truth, truth beauty, — that is all
Ye know on earth, and all ye need to know.

It is perhaps no accident that these lines have been seen as more problematical, and have been more extensively analysed and discussed, than any other passage of Keats's poetry. Unlike the 'sensuous' effects of the poem, these lines appear to propose an idea; so we can't just respond with spontaneous pleasure to an emotional communication, we must receive the idea — as a confirmation perhaps, or maybe as a challenge, but certainly as something questionable, to be considered. Leavis's critical approach blends the sensuous and the ideological together, so that the vividness and power of the former are sufficient to convey the objective truth of the latter.

In addition to this contradiction within the descriptive theory of language, linguistic science has in recent times begun to question very fundamentally the assumption that there is a direct and stable relationship between language and the 'real world' it represents. We tend to assume that there is a 'natural' relationship between a word and the thing that word denotes, an almost physical similarity between name and thing: so that naming the thing in language is almost tantamount to perceiving or even possessing it. Linguists have demonstrated that there is no such natural connection between word and object: different languages for example employ quite different sounds to denote the same object. So the relationship between language and reality is a matter of usage and convention: we grow accustomed to the physical properties of words, and their association with the things they refer to becomes a matter of familiar experience, only *apparently* 'natural'. What this means is that the processes by which we learn to relate language and world, the processes of socialisation and schooling, have much more influence over the way in which we perceive the world through language than the inherent properties of language itself. And the relationship between words and what they signify is in an important sense arbitrary: fixed by social convention, perhaps manipulated by powerful interest-groups within a society.

The implications for Leavis's critical method of such theories of language is that the method will no longer work: since the words in a poem which appear to depict with an almost physical texture real objects and events, are in reality constructing abstract images of a world in language. There is no one-to-one correspondence between words and the things they name, but a gap which is filled with meaning by the social processes of linguistic usage. This 'slippage' between language and reality means that the words of a poem are much more open to interpretation than they are in Leavis's criticism: 'the wealth of globed peonies' might mean many different things to different people in different situations; and some of those meanings might have little to do with any direct physical encounter with a flower.

I have been talking about this disturbance in the formerly stable relationship between language and reality in terms of modern linguistics. I am not suggesting however that an aware-ness of that disturbance was not available to thinkers and writers before these ideas became current in the late twentieth century. Like most theories of language, this one was intuited and anticipated many times by those most concerned with the possibilities and limitations of language — writers; among them, John Keats. This very problem of the stability and continuity of meaning is addressed directly in stanza 7 of the 'Ode to a Nightingale':

> Thou wast not born for death, immortal Bird!
>   No hungry generations tread thee down;
> The voice I hear this passing night was heard
>   In ancient days by emperor and clown:
> Perhaps the self-same song that found a path
>   Through the sad heart of Ruth, when, sick for home,
>   She stood in tears amid the alien corn

The 'immortality' of the nightingale consists, not in some spiri-tual immunity to death, but in the continuity of experience embodied in the history of its song. The music of the nightingale has held the same *meaning* for generation after generation of human beings: in the pleasure and sadness, the ecstasy and yearning of perishable mortals, this thing of beauty remains a constant possession. The elusive object of the poem's quest seems here to be attained: the poet has transcended his imprisoning self-hood to a sympathetic contemplation of other lives; he has resolved the contradictions between life and beauty; he has reconciled his painful love for life with his sensuous desire for death. The nightingale is netted in an intricate web of language: in the poem's music, the spirit of beauty is integrated with a concern for humanity, so that beauty and truth are one.

But what precisely is the nature of the experience that the poem has grasped? It is not a sense of possessing the world, holding it firm like a solid object cupped in the hand; but a melancholy desire for a world that is always elsewhere: home-sickness, longing, yearning for what is not. The common experi-ence that the poem grasps, is that what human beings have in common is an overwhelming and inconsolable sense of loss, of 'alienation', of not being where they belong. As the language of the poem seizes at reality, it discovers reality as absent, deferred, the longed-for and wished-for unattainable. What at one moment seems present and real, comes a moment later to seem like a receding illusion:

> Adieu! the fancy cannot cheat so well
> As she is fam'd to do, deceiving elf.
> Adieu! adieu! thy plaintive anthem fades
> Past the near meadows, over the still stream,
> Up the hill-side; and now 'tis buried deep
> In the next valley-glades

(stanza 8)

'Fled is that music': the pretensions of language to bring reality to us are hollow; on the contrary, it can seem to dispel reality, offering in its place an illusory satisfaction, leaving us heavy with unfulfilled desire.

In fact this emphasis on the essentially unattainable nature of reality is a recurrent emphasis throughout the odes, and in this respect Keats's poetry seems to have much more in common with modern thinking about language than with the descriptive view of language that underpinned Leavis's arguments. In the 'Ode on a Grecian Urn' the vase stands for the perfect medium of art, finer than poetry:

> Heard melodies are sweet, but those unheard
> Are sweeter . . .

(stanza 2)

because its visual language can achieve a more perfect realisation of human experience, reconciling the nostalgia of
mortality with the beauty of the eternal:

> Bold Lover, never, never canst thou kiss,
> Though winning near the goal — yet do not grieve;
> She cannot fade, though thou hast not thy bliss,
> For ever wilt thou love, and she be fair!
>
> (stanza 2)

Again, as in the concluding stanzas of the 'Ode to a Nightingale', the reality that the work of art can possess consists more
of yearning and unsatisfied desire than of solid satisfaction in
the palpable grasp of truth. Contemplation of this perfect image
of reality doesn't put the poet in secure possession of the
sensuous world he desires, but rather brings home to him the
evident absence of the object of his desire:

> More happy love! more happy, happy love!
> For ever warm and still to be enjoy'd,
> For ever panting, and for ever young;
> All breathing human passion far above,
> That leaves a heart high-sorrowful and cloy'd,
> A burning forehead, and a parching tongue.

Lastly we can consider 'To Autumn', which is known of all the
odes as the perfect embodiment of concrete, sensuous experience:

> To bend with apples the moss'd cottage-trees,
> And fill all fruit with ripeness to the core;
> To swell the gourd, and plump the hazel shells
> With a sweet kernel . . .
>
> (stanza 1)

The verse here is clearly an illustration of Keats's sensuous
language: words are clustered and clumped together into an
almost clotted texture ('moss'd cottage-trees'), evoking a tactile
solidity of physical being. Yet again, the world that is grasped
is seized at the moment of its passing. Like the sensuous joys
of the 'Ode on Melancholy':

> . . . Beauty that must die;
> And Joy, whose hand is ever at his lips
> Bidding adieu . . .
>
> (stanza 3)

the beauty of autumn is a moment of dying, termination, closure. The basic pattern of the poem, for all its luxurious absorption in the physical sensations of autumn, is a melancholy and nostalgic resignation to absence and loss. Life and vitality, the reality of desire, are elsewhere — 'What are the songs of spring?' — and the closing movement of the poem, with its recurrent allusions to death — 'soft-dying day', 'wailful choir', 'mourn', 'sinking', dies' — is towards another compelling image of alienation:

> And gathering swallows twitter in the skies.

The swallows gather in order to migrate: like the homesick Ruth in the 'Ode to a Nightingale', or the lover in the 'Ode on a Grecian Urn' whose bliss is always denied him, the swallows of 'To Autumn' know instinctively that their true home is elsewhere, and yearn towards it with a restless longing.

Keats's preoccupation with the impossibility of possessing reality seems a peculiarly 'modern' characteristic, compatible not only with recent developments in the study of language, but also with much modern philosophy. Yet it is completely a historical product of its time. The romantic period was, like the Renaissance, an age of enormous discovery and creation, the enlargement of human possibility and power; and an age which could be disabled by an inconsolable sense of rupture and loss. Hamlet testifies to this contradiction in the earlier culture: 'What a piece of work is a man ... And yet to me what is this quintessence of dust?' Like Hamlet, Keats struggled with the problem of finding a language that could adequately map and measure the reality of the world around him; and like Hamlet, he continually rediscovered the truth that language perpetually promises a grip on the world which it never seems to fulfil. What we grasp is always somewhere else; what we possess is already gone. The 'sensuousness' of Keats's poetic language is a heroic attempt to stabilise and appropriate an elusive and ultimately unattainable reality.

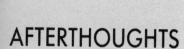

AFTERTHOUGHTS

1

What do you understand by 'sensuousness' (page 91)?

2

How useful do you find the references to the ideas of Leavis in this essay?

3

Do you agree that experience is something 'we all have in common' (page 94)?

4

What is Holderness's view of the relationship between language and experience in Keats's poetry?

Peter Weston

Peter Weston is Dean of the Faculty of
Arts and Humanities at the Roehampton
Institute of Higher Education, and the
author of the Penguin Masterstudy on
Paradise Lost *(1986).*

ESSAY

'Hyperion' and 'The Fall of Hyperion': progress through suffering

'On Monday 21 September 1818, Keats plunged into the most amazingly creative year that any English poet has achieved. Two great unfinished poems on the same theme, "Hyperion" and "The Fall of Hyperion", mark the opening and the close of this period, to the very same day of the year. In this exact year, Keats wrote, with numerous other works, practically every poem that places him among the major poets of the world.' So writes Robert Gittings, Keats's biographer, in his book *John Keats: The Living Year* (London, 1954). Keats was twenty-three in the October of 1818; he died when he was twenty-five, February 1821. An unfinished poem by a major poet is always intriguing, but an unfinished poem together with an unfinished revision, framing as they do in this case a year of intense creativity near the premature end of a young poet's life, is of exceptional interest. What meanings can we find in these texts, both in relation to their contexts and to each other?

In 'Hyperion' Keats chose to write an epic on a mythological subject — the end of the Golden Age, when earth's first gods, the Titans led by Saturn, were deposed in a revolutionary coup by the Olympians led by Jupiter. We may first note three significant aspects to this decision by Keats, which will help to place the poem in context: (1) that he chose Greek mythology as a subject; (2) that he focused on a revolutionary shift of power; and (3) that he wrote in epic form.

Scenes from Greek mythology were at this time a fashionable part of bourgeois taste, influencing Wedgwood pottery designs (Keats himself wrote an 'Ode on a Grecian Urn'), Regency furniture and architecture, and women's clothes. In 'Hyperion', however, the mythological subject-matter is more than decorative. Its paganism gave Keats the latitude to explore his subject without the constraints of Christianity: there is in the poem no dominating concept of sin, no hell, no Satan, no omnipotent God, such as are to be found in Milton's great English epic, *Paradise Lost*. But, equally important for the reception of the poem in its own time, for a person without a university education (Keats trained as a medical student after leaving school) to have aspirations to be a poet, and, worse, to write on classical mythology, was seen by the literary establishment as more than merely impertinent — it was *politically* unacceptable. The infamous review in the August 1818 issue of *Blackwood's Edinburgh Magazine* savaged Keats's first two books under the title 'The Cockney School of Poetry' (meaning poets without 'learning enough to distinguish between the written language of Englishmen and the spoken jargon of Cockneys'), and referred to the 'Cockney school of versification, morality, and politics', claiming that Keats had 'already learned to lisp sedition'.

So for Keats to write about a revolution, although in mythological form, was significant. Keats was politically liberal and progressive, at a time when, following the defeat of Napoleon at Waterloo, England had one of the most repressive governments in its history. England had had its revolution under Cromwell in the 1640s and '50s, which effectively ended feudalism, and had produced its great epic poet, John Milton, whose *Paradise Lost* was the story of the first great rebellions in heaven and on earth. France had had its earth-shaking revolution in 1789 — a generation before Keats was writing — which had led to virtually twenty-two years of war between England

and France, and the conservative reaction to it had produced what seemed like a 'private' epic in Wordsworth's long poem *The Excursion* (1815). Now Keats began writing an epic, in which the setting is the aftermath of a revolution.

No writer who chose the form of epic at this time could avoid writing in the towering shadow of Milton, but the immense Miltonic influence in 'Hyperion' only serves to emphasise the radical difference in Keats's real subject. Milton's *Paradise Lost* opens in Hell, with Satan and his followers on a fiery lake following their *unsuccessful* rebellion against the omnipotent. Satan wakes them with proud, inspirational rhetoric, proposing 'study of revenge, immortal hate,/ And courage never to submit or yield' (Book I, ll.107–108). Other fallen angels are introduced, and they debate strategy. Moloch argues for aggression against God, which will, he says, give the satisfaction of revenge if not of victory; Belial argues for endurance rather than to risk destruction, since God can read their thoughts anyway; and Mammon argues, extending Belial's position, that they should invest in Hell and make it a magnificent place. Finally they agree to follow Beelzebub's advice to search out God's new creation, Adam and Eve, and destroy it. Satan volunteers for the mission, and by the end of Book II he has arrived at the edge of the universe.

'Hyperion' opens with a quite different atmosphere, in deliberate contrast with Milton's poem. Milton's articulate, active, rebellious Satan has become the still, aged, Saturn, sitting in silent depression in a secluded vale. He is not the leader of an unsuccessful rebellion but the victim of a deposition. Thea, wife of the sun-god Hyperion, comes to comfort him, but herself weeps, placing her hand on 'that aching spot/ Where beats the human heart, as if just there,/ Though an immortal, she felt cruel pain' — a sign that the immortal gods are becoming mortal (Book I, ll.42–44). Saturn feels a crisis of identity as, with poignancy and passion, he attempts unsuccessfully to assert his authority and regain his power. Thea conducts him to the other fallen gods in the hope of encouraging them to stand firm. Only Hyperion has not yet fallen, and, pacing his magnificent palace (compare the devils' palace of Pandaemonium in *Paradise Lost*), he threatens to 'scare that infant thunderer, rebel Jove,/ And bid old Saturn take his throne again' (Book

I, ll.249–250). First, however, he comes to earth, on the instruction of Coelus, the omnipresent force of nature.

Book II of 'Hyperion' opens with the arrival of Saturn and Thea at the dark place where the deposed Titans are mourning their loss, surrounded by waterfalls and huge cliffs. (Keats had been on a walking tour of Scotland in July 1818, and the imagery here may derive in part from this experience in the same way as the imagery of Milton's Hell may derive in part from Milton's visit to volcanic regions in Italy.) Saturn discusses strategy with the fallen Titans: he tells them that he can find no reason in history or nature why this downfall should have happened. In a stunning speech, Oceanus encourages a wise endurance: 'We fall by course of Nature's law, not force/ Of thunder, or of Jove', he argues (Book II, ll.181–182). 'The pain of truth' is, he says, that life involves change, but it is only pain to those who resist, because the change he refers to, which has involved their deposition, is a kind of *progress*: 'So on our heels a fresh perfection treads,/ A power more strong in beauty, born of us/ And fated to excel us' (Book II, ll.202, 212–214). Here, with this expression of a faith in 'natural' process, we come close to the central theme of the poem. Oceanus' daughter Clymene speaks next of her feelings on hearing an enchanting melody, which made her 'sick/ Of joy and grief at once', and which was sung by the new god of song (and poetry, therefore), Apollo (Book II, ll.288–289). The final speaker is, by contrast, the wrathful Enceladus, who scorns the 'baby-words' of the previous speakers, and, like Milton's Moloch, advocates aggressive revenge against Jove — at which moment, in a glorious burst of light, Hyperion arrives, and all present acclaim the name of 'Saturn'.

The third, unfinished, book of the poem changes the scene to a Greek island. Apollo is wandering by a rivulet, weeping with an inexplicable sadness, when he is approached by Mnemosyne, the goddess of memory and mother of the muses. She has watched over him all his life, she tells him, and their conversation brings him to the sudden realisation that his 'aching ignorance' is being displaced by 'knowledge enormous', which is making him immortal (Book III, ll.107, 113). He convulsively 'die[s] into life', and the true poet is born. Here the manuscript ends. Keats published the fragment with other poems in July 1820, and the Whig *Monthly Review* thought it the best of the volume.

How are we, then, to understand this text? We have noted the close parallels with *Paradise Lost*, in the situation of defeated gods debating stategy, and coming up with similar proposals in both poems, but there is a crucial difference in that, in Keats's pagan poem, it is the *established authorities* which are defeated by successful rebellion. The central speech by Oceanus, with its wise resignation to a sense of 'progress', is quite different from the essential position of *Paradise Lost*, which proposes that rebellion is sinful, and that perpetual solitary, moral struggle is the necessary task for the Christian. Further, the deification of the poet in the form of Apollo, who understands through memory the meaning of history, is not analogous to anything in Milton — though it does reflect the romantic poets' view of Milton himself, the supremely great, omniscient, epic poet. It is Keats's view of 'suffering' and his view of 'progress' that are crucial here, and these are clarified in certain key letters which he wrote during 1818 and 1819.

On 3 May 1818 Keats wrote to his friend John Hamilton Reynolds about a literary problem: 'whether Miltons apparently less anxiety for Humanity proceeds from his seeing further or no than Wordsworth'. He stresses the importance of feeling, arguing that to be fully understood, ideas about life must be 'proved upon our pulses', so that in the end (half-quoting Byron) '"Sorrow is Wisdom"'. Then, during a famous passage in which he compares human life to a 'large Mansion of Many Apartments', he argues that 'Wordsworth is deeper than Milton', but that at the same time 'Milton as a Philosopher had sure as great powers as Wordsworth'. The reason for this apparent paradox is the concept of *progress*. The greater depth of the modern writer, Wordsworth, was more the result of 'the general and gregarious advance of intellect' than of his individual greatness. Though Milton's Protestantism was a liberating force which freed people from superstition and was progressive in its time, Wordsworth now thinks directly 'into the human heart'. This is evidence for 'a grand march of intellect —; It proves that a mighty providence subdues the mightiest Minds to the service of the time being'. Sixteen months later, Keats elaborated this concept of 'progress' in his journal letter to his brother and sister-in-law George and Georgiana in America on 18 September 1819. He wrote that 'all civil[is]ed countries become gradually more enlighten'd and there should be a continual change for the better'. After a survey of British history he found evidence of a change for the better in the opposition to French tyranny by liberal writers of France and England which culminated in the French Revolution. Though this had an unlucky outcome in the current English government's attempt to restrict freedom and thus prevent change for the better, the very distresses caused to the English people by this policy have roused them to resist, so perhaps, he concludes, the distresses 'are a fortunate thing — tho so horrid in the[i]r experience'. So 'progress' for Keats is a struggle, with advances and reverses, though it carries an inevitability in the long run.

But the struggle can be 'horrid', and to see why for Keats 'progress' does not mean 'perfectibility' we need to investigate his attitude, philosophically speaking, to *suffering*. In an earlier letter to George and Georgiana, written on 21 April 1819, Keats refers to two books he had been reading — one a history of America, the other about Louis XIV. The first was therefore essentially about people uncontaminated by civilisation, and the second about a highly sophisticated courtly society, but what struck Keats most forcibly was that both were full of miseries. However, the Christian idea of this world as a 'vale of tears' from which we may be whisked off to heaven by an arbitrary act of God is for him far too narrow and inadequate a notion. He proposes that, rather, we should think of life in this way:

> Suppose a rose to have sensation, it blooms on a beautiful morning it enjoys itself — but there comes a cold wind, a hot sun — it cannot escape it, it cannot destroy its annoyances — they are as native to the world as itself: no more can man be happy in spite, the world[l]y elements will prey upon his nature.

So, since the context of suffering is part of life which makes us what we are, the world could be called, Keats suggests, 'The vale of Soul-making', where mind (or, intelligence), heart, and world interact to form a soul:

> Do you not see how necessary a World of Pains and troubles is to school an Intelligence and make it a soul? A Place where the

heart must feel and suffer in a thousand diverse ways! ... the Heart ... is the teat from which the Mind or intelligence sucks its identity ... This appears to me a faint sketch of a system of Salvation which does not affront our reason and humanity.

These letters may help us to see one central thrust of 'Hyperion'. Saturn, the deposed man of power, flounders when progress overtakes him, and becomes a victim of suffering. That kind of egocentric identity, unschooled by suffering, is useless: 'I have left/ My strong identity, my real self,/ Somewhere between the throne, and where I sit/ Here on this spot of earth', he laments (Book I, ll.113–116). Oceanus, on the other hand, does have a concept of progress, and advocates disinterestedly facing up to the fact of change:

> Now comes the pain of truth, to whom 'tis pain;
> O folly! for to bear all naked truths,
> And to envisage circumstance, all calm,
> That is the top of sovereignty. . . .
> Soon on our heels a fresh perfection treads,
> A power more strong in beauty, born of us
> And fated to excel us, as we pass [i.e. 'just as we excel']
> In glory that old Darkness.
>
> (Book II, ll.202–205, 212–215)

This understanding, however, is not enough: it has to be *felt*. Clymene (who is Oceanus' daughter, and later in the myth marries Apollo) *knows* that 'joy is gone,/ And this thing woe crept in among our hearts', but, on hearing Apollo's music, which transcends her own, she for the first time *feels* it: 'my sense was fill'd/ With that new blissful golden melody./ A living death was in each gush of sounds' (Book II, ll.253–254, 279–281). She becomes 'sick/ Of joy and grief at once', just as the true poet gives joy by confronting pain (Book II, ll.288–289). Apollo the singer-poet, however, though able to *feel* sorrow as he weeps and dreams, has no way of *understanding* his sadness: 'I strive to search wherefore I am so sad,' he exclaims, 'In fearless yet in aching ignorance' (Book III, ll.88, 107). What he receives from Mnemosyne, goddess of memory, is knowledge of human suffering, which, together with feeling, makes the artist godlike:

Knowledge enormous makes a God of me.
Names, deeds, grey legends, dire events, rebellions,
Majesties, sovran voices, agonies,
Creations and destroyings, all at once
Pour into the wide hollows of my brain,
And deify me . . .

(Book III, ll.113–118)

At this point, with the deification of Apollo, Keats abandoned the poem, in about April 1819 — the month that he wrote the 'vale of Soul-making' letter. We may speculate about his reasons for this decision. Perhaps, with the Titans defeated and Apollo deified, he felt the climax of his story had already been reached. Perhaps Apollo anyway had an impossibly godlike role to fulfil as the poem had so far constructed it. Perhaps in the light of an 'ideal' Apollonian poetry that was to be capable of accommodating the sufferings of the world in a new formulation (Keats was still grieving over the tragic death of his brother Tom the previous December from tuberculosis), he felt the luxuriating poeticisms of Book III — 'soft warble', 'vermeil hue', 'voluptuous fleeces', 'faint-lipped shells', etc. — to be inadequate. Perhaps he felt it was all too Miltonic in form and phrase. Whatever his reasons, however, he returned to his subject three or four months later, probably in July 1819, and began a thorough revision (though we should remember that he thought the first fragment good enough to publish the following year).

The revision, entitled 'The Fall of Hyperion', involved recasting the poem in a quite different, non-Miltonic form — that of the 'dream-vision' in which the poet/narrator is led by a guide and himself participates in the action. This is a verse tradition that goes back at least to Chaucer, and Keats's use of it was perhaps prompted by his reading of Dante, whose guides in his *Divine Comedy* had been Virgil and Beatrice. In 'The Fall of Hyperion', Keats's guide is called Moneta, who is also addressed on one occasion as Mnemosyne, and, like her, represents memory, and is the mother of the muses. She is, however, a much more powerful, vivid, and sinister figure than Mnemosyne. By placing the action of the poem in the poet's consciousness, the poem becomes much more contemporary in feel than the Miltonic epic form. There is also none of the optimistic faith in 'progress' of the former poem. The form now suggests that the subject of the new poem is more centrally the writer and writing, and it opens with a distinction between self-absorbed 'dreamers' and true poets; in fact, Book I may be read as almost an allegory of how a poet is made.

The narrator finds himself in a strange, paradise-like forest, and comes upon the remains of a banquet (reminding us of Eve's banquet in Book V of *Paradise Lost*). He drinks a potion, after which he swoons — much as the self-absorbed 'dreamer' might become deliriously excited by the sensuous beauties of nature. Waking, he finds himself in an ancient abandoned temple, where there is an altar approached by marble steps. He hears a voice, which turns out to be that of his guide, Moneta, tell him, 'If thou canst not ascend/ These steps, die on that marble where thou art', and, stifled by a chilling numbness, he just manages to reach the lowest stair 'one minute before death' (Canto I, ll.107–108, 132). By thus symbolically confronting his own death he becomes enlightened, since the only ones who can climb the steps are 'those to whom the miseries of the world/ Are misery, and will not let them rest' (Canto I, ll.148–149). Unreflective people who 'sleep away their days' or even those good, socially concerned people who 'Labour for mortal good' have no thought to come there, Moneta tells him (Canto I, ll.151, 159). The 'dreamer' has no useful function: he gives no real benefit to the world, and he even suffers more himself, 'Bearing more woe than all his sins deserve' (Canto I, l.176). But surely, the narrator argues, a poet is 'a sage;/ A humanist, physician to all men,' upon which Moneta distinguishes between the true poet, educated by suffering, who 'pours out a balm upon the World' and the mere 'dreamer'. (Canto I, l.201). (Since some lines and phrases here are repeated — e.g. lines 195–198 and 217–220; 187 and 211 — it appears that this crucial section is in an unfinished state; Keats's friend Richard Woodhouse notes that the author 'seems to have intended to erase' this passage.)

The veiled Moneta then identifies the fallen image of Saturn and promises to enlighten the narrator with knowledge, which will be a wonder to him, though without pain for him: he is going to behold the past, the story of the fall of the Titans. At this she parts her veils, and in her face we confront the impersonal stoicism that knowledge of endless suffering has brought:

>   . . . Then saw I a wan face,
> Not pin'd by human sorrows, but bright-blanch'd
> By an immortal sickness which kills not;
> It works a constant change, which happy death
> Can put no end to; deathwards progressing
> To no death was that visage; it had past
> The lily and the snow; and beyond these
> I must not think now, though I saw that face —
> But for her eyes I should have fled away.
> They held me back, with a benignant light,
> Soft-mitigated by divinest lids
> Half-closed, and visionless entire they seem'd
> Of all external things; — they saw me not,
> But in blank splendor beam'd like the mild moon,
> Who comforts those she sees not, who knows not
> What eyes are upward cast.

(Canto I, ll.256–271)

This symbolises the role of the true poet: impersonal, immortal, compelling and comforting. From Keats's analogy with the 'vale of Soul-making' we understand that suffering educates the heart and mind, so true poetry is not escapism or dreaming, not self-centred effusion, but a 'balm upon the World' in its informed objectivity (Canto I, l.201). Here Keats is moving towards the post-romantic conception of the impersonality of art that so preoccupied later writers such as W B Yeats.

From this point onwards, 'deep in the shady sadness of a vale' (l.294), the narrator recounts the story of 'Hyperion' as it is revealed to him in the present and in the first person. This is the 'high tragedy/ In the dark secret chambers of her [i.e. Moneta's] skull' (Canto I, l.277–278). Saturn in this version is, however, full of despair, uttering twelve injunctions to 'moan', so that the narrator comments 'Methought I heard some old man of the earth/ Bewailing earthly loss' (Canto I, ll.440–441). His sorrows reflect the sorrows of humanity, and without the hope that his speech in 'Hyperion' articulated. In the earlier poem the description of the heavens in Saturn's speech leads to an expectation of the arrival of Hyperion 'to repossess/ A heaven he lost erewhile', but now the stars lead Saturn to the destructive thought: 'There is no death in all the Universe,/ No smell of death — there shall be death — Moan, moan'. ('Hyperion' Book I, ll.123–124; 'The Fall of Hyperion' Canto I, ll.423–424). His earlier semi-hopeful self-questioning — 'But cannot I create?/ Cannot I form? Cannot I fashion forth / Another world, another universe [?]' — is in the new version now missing ('Hyperion' Book I, ll.141–143).

And again the poem breaks off. Keats gives an explanation for this in a letter to Reynolds, dated 21 September 1819, in which he writes 'I have given up Hyperion–there were too many Miltonic inversions in it . . . I wish to give myself up to other sensations.' Whether this is the whole explanation, or what these 'other sensations' were, we can only speculate. It is, however, noteworthy that two days before writing these words he had composed his great ode 'To Autumn', with its sensuous evocation of the fecundity and sad joy in seasonal change, and its imaginative representation of life as an inclusive and valuable whole.

Compared with 'Hyperion', 'The Fall of Hyperion' is a poem of inwardness and doubt. It is not possible to 'explain' the differences between the two poems through examination of specific experiences or events during Keats's creative year. Certainly by the end of this year, simple strategies for coming to terms with suffering, such as a faith in some kind of collective 'progress' or a reliance on 'dreaming' through art, seem quite inadequate, and 'The Fall of Hyperion' lays an almost impossible burden on the poet: to provide consolation for humanity he/she must aspire to the grave serenity of Moneta in accepting the necessity of pain to the formation of the soul. Despite Moneta's promise that he will feel no pain in observing the story of the fall of the Titans, we may note that the narrator *does* in fact intensely wish 'that death would take me from the Vale' (Canto I, ll.248, 397). But there is no escape, for the poet or for anyone: there is only the redeeming knowledge that whatever we might be is the result of accommodating to the native condition of shared humanity, as the rose comes to terms with the cold wind, the hot sun.

AFTERTHOUGHTS

1

What reasons are advanced in this essay for Keats's interest in the Hyperion legend?

2

Does a reader need to know Milton's poetry to appreciate these two poems?

3

What does Weston highlight as the significant differences between the two poems?

4

Both poems confront the problem of suffering: what solutions do they offer?

John Creaser

*John Creaser is Hildred Carlile
Professor of English at the University of
London, and Head of the English
Department at Royal Holloway and
Bedford New College. He is the author of
numerous scholarly works.*

ESSAY

Saying and meaning in 'To Autumn'

Until a generation ago, Keats's ode 'To Autumn' was loved and yet patronised as no more than an exquisite description of nature, as an almost flawless piece of writing with nothing to say. It is now judged to be one of the greatest and richest of Keats's poems, and one of the central texts of the romantic period. How is it that a poem which *says* so little can *mean* so much?

Superficially, the poem does bear out the older reading. By Keatsian standards, its structure and style are straightforward to the point of austerity. In outline, it is no more than a series of lists, moving from autumnal ripeness to autumnal tasks and to autumnal sounds — first before, then during and finally just after harvest — and moving in parallel from the sense of touch to sight and then to hearing. It seems to lack the vitality of both reflection and poetic effect, and also the sense of urgent individuality, which characterise the other great odes; it lacks the vivid Keatsian repertoire of allusion to classical mythology and art and modern literature; the language of thought is scarcely present, and there is not a single first-person pronoun.

Yet Keats, I am sure, would have deplored the older reading. The immediate inspiration of the ode was a walk among stubble-fields near Winchester on Sunday, 19 September 1819; the poem was probably drafted the same day, and the text took shape so quickly that a copy could be sent to a friend on Tuesday the 21st. The day before the walk, Keats wrote to his brother and sister-in-law, George and Georgina: 'For myself I hate descriptions', and the day after the walk he distinguished himself from Byron by adding: 'He describes what he sees — I describe what I imagine.' A moment's reflection will reveal how selective an account of the season the poem really is. Moreover, most of the vivid descriptions prove on examination to have a *mental* existence: the first stanza does not describe ripe fruit but invokes an Autumn who is planning *how* to ripen fruit; the appearances of Autumn in the second stanza and the sunset in the third are recollected and typical scenes; only the last two and a half lines of the poem present a direct experience.

Finally, there is the addressing of the poem to a deified Autumn. An abstraction is personified — given the attributes of life — and projected onto the portrayal of natural fecundity. The artificiality of this bothered earlier readers; the poet Robert Bridges, for example, thought it a blemish that the words 'Think not of them' are 'somewhat awkwardly addressed to a personification of Autumn'.[1] It seemed to make the description less real.

It is worth reflecting why a personified aspect of nature should be so prominent in a major romantic work. It gives the poem an outmoded and even archaic quality, since it harks back to an older form of the ode and of landscape poetry against which the romantics had reacted.

Poets have not always been rigorous in their use of the term 'ode', but essentially an ode is the most exalted of lyric forms. Its tone is serious, its form often elaborate, its structure and rhythm stately. It is usually addressed to a higher being — hero, king, or deity — and often takes some current occasion as a base for public, reflective or philosophic writing. It is a ceremonious and celebratory form, expressing a mind which is fired by enthusiasm but concerned to maintain dignity and decorum. It originated in the cult-hymns of the ancient world, which began by

---

[1] Robert Bridges, *John Keats: A Critical Essay* (1895); see G S Fraser (ed.), *Keats: Odes* (Macmillan Casebook, 1971), p.54.

invoking the presence of a deity, continued with a detailed celebration of the acts which demonstrated the god's powers and virtues, and ended with renewed invocation in the form of a prayer. Fine ancient reworkings of the form include Sappho's hymn or prayer to Aphrodite and Cleanthes' 'Hymn to Zeus', but the mark of its enthusiastic fervour of invocation is clear in many modern poems, such as Shelley's 'Ode to the West Wind', which was also written in the autumn of 1819.[2]

The exalted vehemence of the ode was highly valued in the eighteenth century, and from around 1740 the form was attempted by almost all poets, most successfully by Thomas Gray and William Collins, whose work Keats certainly knew. The period developed a distinctive kind of ode, unified around an address to a single personification, such as Gray's 'Ode on the Spring' and 'Ode to Adversity' or Collins's 'Ode to Evening' and 'Ode to Peace'. The poems are not only organised around one personification but often populated by incidental personifications with allegorical attributes.

The major romantics reacted strongly against this tradition, especially its personification of nature. For the contemporaries of Gray and Collins, personification could fuse an intellectual control of experience with imaginative and even visionary intensity. To Wordsworth, Coleridge and their successors, it seemed merely a meretricious ornament. In Wordsworth's Preface to *Lyrical Ballads*, personification is dismissed as the first vice of style, of 'the gaudiness and inane phraseology of many modern writers'. In chapter XVIII of *Biographia Literaria*, the most ambitious critical text of the age, Coleridge disdains the hysteria of the previous century's 'sundry odes and apostrophes to abstract terms'. Not merely a feature of style but a whole view of life was at issue. Romantic intuitions of One Life

---

[2] The celebrated poems by Sappho (*fl.* 600 BC) and Cleanthes (331–232 BC) are reprinted and translated in Constantine A Trypanis (ed.), *The Penguin Book of Greek Verse* (Harmondsworth, 1971), pp.144 and 283. The standard account of the English ode in relation to the ancient cult-hymn is in German, Kurt Schlüter, *Die Englische Ode* (Bonn, 1964), but his findings are summarised in the course of a fine essay by Geoffrey H Hartman, 'Poem and Ideology: A Study in Keats's "To Autumn"', reprinted in his collection *The Fate of Reading and Other Essays* (Chicago, 1975), pp.124–146.

flowing through all creation, and of what Wordsworth terms an 'ennobling interchange' between nature and the human mind, were incompatible with the manifest and traditional artifice of a personified nature. In the romantic period, therefore, the ode to an abstraction is supplanted by poems such as Coleridge's 'Frost at Midnight' and Wordsworth's 'Tintern Abbey' or ode on 'Intimations of Immortality', where a given speaker moves between a specific landscape and a decisive process of meditation and feeling, constantly interrelating the self and the not-self as his understanding deepens.[3]

Why, then, should Keats have employed so anachronistic a method in 'To Autumn'? Why should he choose not to re-create but certainly to echo the eighteenth-century ode and personify an aspect of nature, especially in a poem which elsewhere is straightforward in its planning and richly intimate with natural processes?

Provisionally, it can be said that it brings a sense of benign providence into those processes. The first two stanzas evoke an earthly paradise within our fallen world and create an ideal relation between nature and man, with all nature's fecundity as harvest in the service of man. The world of generation is seen in a state of beatitude, where plenitude never spills into over-ripeness, burst shells and broken branches. The only excess is the mellow 'o'er-brimming' of the bees' cells; the only mortal consciousness is their sense of unending summer. All the bliss of the year seems condensed into this enchanted period of fulfilment just before repletion.

The first stanza almost annuls time; it lacks a main verb, and the consequent lack of syntactic impetus allures us into lingering on instance after instance of fruition. The second stanza is clearly and symmetrically structured, yet maintains a sense of effortless amplitude. Animation is suspended, and the busiest and most anxious phase of the agricultural year becomes a delicious absent-mindedness and abandonment. Only one of

---

[3] For an authoritative account of this distinctive form, see M H Abrams, 'Structure and Style in the Greater Romantic Lyric', in Frederick W Hilles and Harold Bloom (eds), *From Sensibility to Romanticism: Essays Presented to Frederick A. Pottle* (London, 1965), pp.527–560.

the four manifestations of Autumn is in motion, and 'she' communicates a feeling of poise and equilibrium, not of back-breaking toil.

The figure of Autumn brings intimations of divinity into this earthly paradise. It is Autumn's 'conspiring' which breathes such potency into nature. It is because of Autumn that the laden branches of the fruit trees and the laden head of the 'gleaner' are felt as a blessing and not a burden. Moreover, the second stanza adds subtle hints of divine revelation to the earthly beatitude. The stanza has a biblical resonance, amplified by the echo of the Sermon on the Mount in line 13: 'whoever seeks abroad may find. . .', recalling 'Ask, and it shall be given you; seek, and ye shall find' (Matthew 7:7; Luke 11:9). Christ's utterance affirms God's unstinted bounty towards man, and similarly the freely visible manifestations of Autumn embody the gracious presence of the divine among the earthly.[4]

Keats both evokes and defuses the biblical terrors of divine revelation and judgement, which so frequently employ images of harvest. Here the deity does not winnow the worthless chaff from the good corn but is 'herself' winnowed — 'thy hair soft-lifted by the winnowing wind' — and the reaper is anything but grim. Autumn evokes a human life in touch with the divine, unburdened by the Fall and all its consequent misery, sacrifice, and judgement — a theology which Keats thought an affront to reason and humanity.[5]

The fiction of a personified Autumn enables Keats, then, to incorporate a caring godhead into natural process. Paradoxically, it also enables him to annul that godhead. In this way 'To Autumn' resembles Keats's great series of odes written in the spring of 1819 more closely than some critics have perceived. In 'Ode to a Nightingale', for example, the speaker attempts to

---

[4] The echo of the Gospels is noted in Helen Vendler, *The Odes of John Keats* (London, 1983), p.250. Although sometimes erratic, her chapter on 'To Autumn' is the most searching critique the poem has received.

[5] See letter to George and Georgina Keats, 21 April 1819, in which he outlines a vision of the world as a 'vale of Soul-making' and is dismissive of Christian redemption. See also Robert Gittings, *John Keats* (Harmondsworth, 1971), pp.521–523.

exalt the bird into embodying a state of timeless perfection —
'not born for death' — but again and again he is disenchanted by
the stubborn honesty of 'the dull brain'. In 'To Autumn', intuitions
of a numinous and gracious presence in nature, enveloping
human life, are tellingly evoked and negated.

In the first stanza, for example, the traditional deification
is swamped in natural phenomena. This is why generations of
readers took the figure of Autumn almost for granted. As the
unshaped syntax stretches on and on, the orthodox invocation
of a superior being loses direction. Autumn's 'conspiring' is felt
as the immediate presentation of natural process, and by the end
of the stanza we have moved imperceptibly from providence into
real time: 'For summer *has* o'er-brimm'd . . .'. In the second
stanza, the series of figures hints at Christian revelation and
also at Ceres, the ancient goddess of corn and of harvest.[6] Yet
in the final effect, deity is displaced into manifestations of care-
free human life. Poppies were sacred to Ceres, while the reaper
is 'drowsed' by them. Where we might expect a divine being
with traces of the human, we perceive human beings released
from laboriousness and sorrow.

Autumn is never more present, nor more emphatically
absent, than in the final stanza. The intimate address of the
opening lines may seem to establish the presence of a venerated
being, yet the notion that a seasonal deity might need such
reassurance is bizarre. The 'awkwardness' on which Bridges
commented has point. Its self-consciousness makes us aware
that the deity which has earlier been displaced into natural
process and into human life has now been absorbed into the
poet; he is attempting to reassure *himself*. For two matchless
stanzas, he has celebrated a paradisial world, as if seeking to
persuade himself of its adequacy. But it is only the bees which
'think warm days will never cease'; the 'next swath' remains the
next for cutting, and the 'last oozings' must fall at last. Time
will not relent, and suddenly in the third stanza we find the
harvest is already over; the poem of fruition has been uttered
from the stubble-plains.

Our abrupt awareness of the speaker in what had seemed

---

[6] See Ian Jack, *Keats and the Mirror of Art* (Oxford, 1967), p.236.

an impersonal and undramatic poem is the moment of 'cold pastoral' — that disenchanted questioning of the image of perfection which marks the odes of 1819. By advising against thought of the songs of spring, the speaker *makes* us think of them. By consoling the season so implausibly, he makes us aware of his own need for consolation. The tone is quite different from the autumnal serenity of the letter, written on 21 September 1819 to his friend John Hamilton Reynolds, in which Keats first mentions the poem:

> How beautiful the season is now — How fine the air. A temperate sharpness about it. Really, without joking, chaste weather — Dian skies — I never lik'd stubble fields so much as now — Aye better than the chilly green of the spring. Somehow a stubble plain looks warm — in the same way that some pictures look warm — This struck me so much in my sunday's walk that I composed upon it.

By recalling the matchless songs rather than the 'chilly green' of spring, the poem injects a feeling of loss into the comparison of the seasons. And as the speaker seeks to come to terms with that loss, the figure of Autumn drops from his mind and disappears. The vital third phase of an ode to a superior being or presence — the renewed invocation and prayer — is simply ignored, as the speaker adjusts himself to earthly considerations, moving from what happens 'oft' (1.12) to 'then' (1.27) to 'now' (1.31), his present reality.

Such consolation as he can find among the stubble merely sharpens the poignancy of loss; the rosy 'bloom' of springtime youth is now the fleeting beauty of sunset. It is only too clear that autumn's 'music' of wailing, bleating, and twittering cannot match the songs of spring, and though the autumnal sounds are loved, they are redolent of death — the mourning choir floats or sinks as the wind 'lives or dies'; the day is 'soft-dying'. It is the end of a day at the end of harvest; winter is the eloquent absence implied throughout the stanza, and the seasonal 'gathering' is now of swallows for migration rather than of corn for the granary. The most musical sound is the whistling of the robin, pre-eminently the bird of winter.

Yet this final stanza's process of disenchantment and its elegiac feeling of transience and mortality lead to no ironic or embittered disillusionment, to no reaction which might diminish the beauties of nature. The personification of Autumn portrayed an attempt to find a consoling fiction of providential concern within nature. Its displacement, the demythologising of Autumn into autumn in the course of the poem, leaves the poet contemplating natural phenomena in themselves. Keats was already impatient of the Church and the Christian hope of redemption. 'To Autumn' further constitutes a denial of an 'ennobling interchange' between man and nature, offering man the perception of One Life in all creation. It is deeply moving that with these two grounds of hope gone, Keats neither dismisses the secularised landscape and season of the poem as inadequate to human need nor appropriates them into a symbol of human experience, reducing them to an image of man's emotions. Critics have found truths such as 'Ripeness is all' or 'Everything that lives is holy' implied within the still, sad music of the closing lines, but Keats is no more prepared to reduce nature to a mere vehicle in this way than he is content simply to enumerate the distinctive endowments of the season.[7]

One can write of Keats in this poem as T S Eliot once wrote of Henry James: his genius 'comes out most tellingly in his mastery over, his baffling escape from, Ideas. . . . He had a mind so fine that no idea could violate it.'[8] The stanza and its landscape do not exist in order to *illustrate* meanings, and hence are not merely embryonic until rounded into an inclusive pattern of meaning. They are pregnant with significances, but lack signification. All the autumnal music suggests process or transience, but the emotional configurations of the lines are manifold and shifting.

Death is suggested, for example, by the 'dying' of the day at sunset, the wailful mourning of the gnats, the fitfulness of the wind and the song of that short-lived creature of summer, the grasshopper; the coming of winter is implied in the presence of stubble, the maturity of the lambs, the song of the red-breast

---

[7] The first phrase is quoted from *King Lear* 5.2.11, and the second occurs repeatedly in Blake's earlier work (see 'A Song of Liberty', 'Visions of the Daughters of Albion', l.215, and 'America', l.71).

[8] Frank Kermode (ed.), *Selected Prose of T. S. Eliot* (London, 1975), p.151.

and the gathering of the swallows. But the 'soft-dying' of the day and the 'treble soft' of the robin preserve the gentleness of the idyll in stanza 2: 'Thy hair soft-lifted by the winnowing wind'. A sense of enclosure and limitation is transformed into a thing of beauty in the sunset's streaks of 'barrèd clouds', or into a sense of liberation in the airy spaciousness of 'hilly bourn'. There is even a trace of affectionate comedy in the transformation of gnats' buzzing into a chorus of death; from the lovely perspective of these stubble-plains it is possible to tease the grim reaper by giving him such tiny prey.

The emotional colouring of each detail is open to diverse although not unlimited interpretation. For example, the phrase 'hedge-crickets sing' lifts the heart with the gaiety of its response to the smaller creatures of nature, and for its recollection of a summery stillness and warmth. Yet does not the verb 'sing' — the most musical verb of the stanza — diminish the musicality which it claims, by making too much of the brisk whirring and chirping of the grasshopper? Moreover, by calling the grasshopper a hedge-*cricket*, Keats is summoning winter to our minds, for the cricket on the hearth had long been one of the distinctive sounds of winter (the comparison between the two seasonal insects is presented in Keats's sonnet 'On the Grasshopper and Cricket'). Yet the wintry forecast need not be gloomy, since that fireside chirping is proverbial for its gaiety — 'as merry as a cricket' — and brings a contented warmth and repose to mind.

Such a *spiral* of meaning inheres in every single phrase of the closing stanza, so that the stanza, and with it the poem, cannot be reduced to one configuration of meaning, however ambiguous. But the diversity is not an unprincipled deviousness, or a retreat into mere indecisiveness. Keats was often aware that the more blunt someone's mind the more easily it could be 'violated' or possessed by an idea, and by a hunger for certainty. He treasured the Shakespearian virtue of tolerant and patient openness which he once termed '*Negative Capability*, that is when man is capable of being in uncertainties, Mysteries, doubts, without any irritable reaching after fact & reason' (letter to George and Tom Keats, 21 December 1817). This was at the forefront of his mind in the days during which he wrote the ode, since in a letter to George and Georgina on 24

September 1819 he said that he had been writing in another letter of his friend Charles Wentworth Dilke:

> a Man who cannot feel he has a personal identity unless he has made up his Mind about every thing. The only means of strengthening one's intellect is to make up ones mind about nothing — to let the mind be a thoroughfare for all thoughts .... Dilke will never come at a truth as long as he lives; because he is always trying at it.

Such passages suggest a strong and persistent feeling for the values of patience, tolerance, intuition, and openness to experience. 'To Autumn' is Keats's most poised achievement of this 'negative capability'; no poem could be less 'irritable', less hungry after 'truth', less anxious to escape doubts and reach the consolation of a sense of conviction. Its achievement lies not in what the ode says, but in the contemplative flexibility of mind, unshaken by its doubts and anxieties, which it makes manifest.

It is this which gives such depth and resonance to the poem's serenity and lack of self-concern. The most pervasive and quietly telling divergence from convention is the ode's lack of vehemence; there is none of the cult-hymn's frenzy of volition. It voices no prayer and makes no demands. There is none of the over-heated yearning of the earlier odes ('More happy love, more happy, happy love!), leading to wishful thinking, or confusion, or painful irony. 'To Autumn' maintains a rapt calm in its contemplation of temporal process. The transient ripeness on which it concentrates is apprehended as the culmination of a cycle — epitomised in the 'full-grown lambs' and 'hedge-crickets', creatures of all seasons. Since its rewards are given through time, they are not rejected as merely evanescent.

Biographically, 'To Autumn' is the product of a brief period of resolution and determination in the middle of what was to prove Keats's last month of unfettered creativity, ending the most creative year any modern poet has known. Keats had long been anxious about his health. Writing and his love for Fanny Brawne were alike fevers to him, and he had pathetic hopes of weaning himself from Fanny and of being able to write out of 'a more thoughtful and quiet power'. He was only too aware how ridiculous the miseries of love could appear, and what ridicule he faced as an idiosyncratic writer at a time when the reviewers were often polemical and vindictive. He was conscious of feelings of personal insignificance, of his morbid brooding, and of his all too 'unsteady & vagarish disposition'. His financial anxieties were chronic, and although his pressing immediate needs had been relieved for the time being early in September, within a few days came desperate news of financial crisis from George and Georgina, who were settlers in America. Keats hurried to London on Friday, 10 September, and there spent a few days making every effort to raise money on George's behalf.

The concentration of meeting a real crisis steadied him — 'Imaginary grievances have always been more my torment than real ones', he wrote to a friend on the 23rd. His vigorous efforts on behalf of his brother and sister-in-law led to a flurry of letters in which he laid plans to earn his independence and self-respect by returning from Winchester to London and making his way in political journalism.[9]

The resolution was soon to be frustrated by deteriorating health, but at least in 'To Autumn' we have one great realisation of his ambitions, one ripe poem of 'a more thoughtful and quiet power'. In its selflessness, its lack of brooding melancholy and its patient withholding of any palpable design upon the reader, 'To Autumn' is a triumph of courageous serenity.

---

[9] The evidence summarised in this and the preceding paragraph is drawn from Keats's letters of August and September, 1819. The period and its letters are, of course, examined at length in any biography of Keats.

AFTERTHOUGHTS

1

Compare the analysis of 'To Autumn' in this essay with Hollindale's account of it on pages 62–63.

2

'How is it that a poem that *says* so little can *mean* so much?' (paragraph one). Do you find this a useful distinction?

3

What do *you* take to be the relationship between Christian and pagan elements in this poem (see pages 117–118)?

4

What does Creaser mean by 'the moment of "cold pastoral"' (page 119)?

A PRACTICAL GUIDE TO ESSAY WRITING

INTRODUCTION

First, a word of warning. Good essays are the product of a creative engagement with literature. So never try to restrict your studies to what you think will be 'useful in the exam'. Ironically, you will restrict your grade potential if you do.

This doesn't mean, of course, that you should ignore the basic skills of essay writing. When you read critics, make a conscious effort to notice *how* they communicate their ideas. The guidelines that follow offer advice of a more explicit kind. But they are no substitute for practical experience. It is never easy to express ideas with clarity and precision. But the more often you tackle the problems involved and experiment to find your own voice, the more fluent you will become. So practise writing essays as often as possible.

HOW TO PLAN
AN ESSAY

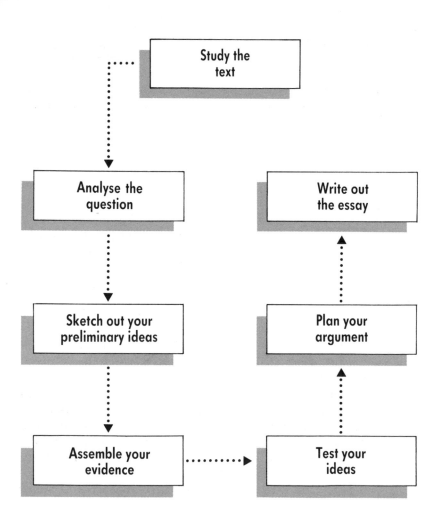

Study the text

The first step in writing a good essay is to get to know the set text well. Never write about a text until you are fully familiar with it. Even a discussion of the opening chapter of a novel, for example, should be informed by an understanding of the book as a whole. Literary texts, however, are by their very nature complex and on a first reading you are bound to miss many significant features. Re-read the book with care, if possible more than once. Look up any unfamiliar words in a good dictionary and if the text you are studying was written more than a few decades ago, consult the *Oxford English Dictionary* to find out whether the meanings of any terms have shifted in the intervening period.

Good books are difficult to put down when you first read them. But a more leisurely second or third reading gives you the opportunity to make notes on those features you find significant. An index of characters and events is often useful, particularly when studying novels with a complex plot or time scheme. The main aim, however, should be to record your *responses* to the text. By all means note, for example, striking images. But be sure to add *why* you think them striking. Similarly, record any thoughts you may have on interesting comparisons with other texts, puzzling points of characterisation, even what you take to be aesthetic blemishes. The important thing is to annotate fully and adventurously. The most seemingly idiosyncratic comment may later lead to a crucial area of discussion which you would otherwise have overlooked. It helps to have a working copy of the text in which to mark up key passages and jot down marginal comments (although obviously these practices are taboo when working with library, borrowed or valuable copies!). But keep a fuller set of notes as well and organise these under appropriate headings.

Literature does not exist in an aesthetic vacuum, however, and you should try to find out as much as possible about the context of its production and reception. It is particularly important to read other works by the same author and writings by contemporaries. At this early stage, you may want to restrict your secondary reading to those standard reference works, such as biographies, which are widely available in public libraries. In the long run, however, it pays to read as wide a range of critical studies as possible.

Some students, and tutors, worry that such studies may stifle the development of any truly personal response. But this won't happen if you are alert to the danger and read critically. After all, you wouldn't passively accept what a stranger told you in conversation. The fact that a critic's views are in print does not necessarily make them any more authoritative (as a glance at the review pages of the *TLS* and *London Review of Books* will reveal). So question the views you find: 'Does this critic's interpretation agree with mine and where do we part company?' 'Can it be right to try and restrict this text's meanings to those found by its author or first audience?' 'Doesn't this passage treat a theatrical text as though it were a novel?' Often it is views which you reject which prove most valuable since they challenge you to articulate your own position with greater clarity. Be sure to keep careful notes on what the critic wrote, and your *reactions* to what the critic wrote.

Analyse the question

You cannot begin to answer a question until you understand what task it is you have been asked to perform. Recast the question in your own words and reconstruct the line of reasoning which lies behind it. Where there is a choice of topics, try to choose the one for which you are best prepared. It would, for example, be unwise to tackle 'How far do you agree that in *Paradise Lost* Milton transformed the epic models he inherited from ancient Greece and Rome?' without a working knowledge of Homer and Virgil (or *Paradise Lost* for that matter!). If you do not already know the works of these authors, the question should spur you on to read more widely — or discourage you from attempting it at all. The scope of an essay, however, is not always so obvious and you must remain alert to the implied demands of each question. How could you possibly 'Consider the view that *Wuthering Heights* transcends the conventions of the Gothic novel' without reference to at least some of those works which, the question suggests, have *not* transcended Gothic conventions?

When you have decided on a topic, analyse the terms of the question itself. Sometimes these self-evidently require careful definition: *tragedy* and *irony*, for example, are notoriously difficult concepts to pin down and you will probably need to consult a good dictionary of literary terms. Don't ignore, however, those seemingly innocuous phrases which often smuggle in significant assumptions. 'Does Macbeth lack the nobility of the true tragic hero?' obviously invites you to discuss nobility and the nature of the tragic hero. But what of 'lack' and 'true' — do they suggest that the play would be improved had Shakespeare depicted Macbeth in a different manner? or that tragedy is superior to other forms of drama? Remember that you are not expected meekly to agree with the assumptions implicit in the question. Some questions are deliberately provocative in order to stimulate an engaged response. Don't be afraid to take up the challenge.

Sketch out your preliminary ideas

'Which comes first, the evidence or the answer?' is one of those chicken and egg questions. How can you form a view without inspecting the evidence? But how can you know which evidence is relevant without some idea of what it is you are looking for? In practice the mind reviews evidence and formulates preliminary theories or hypotheses at one and the same time, although for the sake of clarity we have separated out the processes. Remember that these early ideas are only there to get you started. You *expect* to modify them in the light of the evidence you uncover. Your initial hypothesis may be an instinctive 'gut-reaction'. Or you may find that you prefer to 'sleep on the problem', allowing ideas to gell over a period of time. Don't worry in either case. The mind is quite capable of processing a vast amount of accumulated evidence, the product of previous reading and thought, and reaching sophisticated intuitive judgements. Eventually, however, you are going to have to think carefully through any ideas you arrive at by such intuitive processes. Are they logical? Do they take account of all the relevant factors? Do they fully answer the question set? Are there any obvious reasons to qualify or abandon them?

Assemble your evidence

Now is the time to return to the text and re-read it with the question and your working hypothesis firmly in mind. Many of the notes you have already made are likely to be useful, but assess the precise relevance of this material and make notes on any new evidence you discover. The important thing is to cast your net widely and take into account points which tend to undermine your case as well as those that support it. As always, ensure that your notes are full, accurate, and reflect your own critical judgements.

You may well need to go outside the text if you are to do full justice to the question. If you think that the 'Oedipus complex' may be relevant to an answer on *Hamlet* then read Freud and a balanced selection of those critics who have discussed the appropriateness of applying psychoanalytical theories to the interpretation of literature. Their views can most easily be tracked down by consulting the annotated bibliographies held by most major libraries (and don't be afraid to ask a librarian for help in finding and using these). Remember that you go to works of criticism not only to obtain information but to stimulate you into clarifying your own position. And that since life is short and many critical studies are long, judicious use of a book's index and/or contents list is not to be scorned. You can save yourself a great deal of future labour if you carefully record full bibliographic details at this stage.

Once you have collected the evidence, organise it coherently. Sort the detailed points into related groups and identify the quotations which support these. You must also assess the relative importance of each point, for in an essay of limited length it is essential to establish a firm set of priorities, exploring some ideas in depth while discarding or subordinating others.

Test your ideas

As we stressed earlier, a hypothesis is only a proposal, and one that you fully expect to modify. Review it with the evidence before you. Do you really still believe in it? It would be surprising if you did not want to modify it in some way. If you cannot see any problems, others may. Try discussing your ideas with friends and relatives. Raise them in class discussions. Your tutor is certain to welcome your initiative. The critical process is essentially collaborative and there is absolutely no reason why you should not listen to and benefit from the views of others. Similarly, you should feel free to test your ideas against the theories put forward in academic journals and books. But do not just borrow what you find. Critically analyse the views on offer and, where appropriate, integrate them into your own pattern of thought. You must, of course, give full acknowledgement to the sources of such views.

Do not despair if you find you have to abandon or modify significantly your initial position. The fact that you are prepared to do so is a mark of intellectual integrity. Dogmatism is never an academic virtue and many of the best essays explore the *process* of scholarly enquiry rather than simply record its results.

Plan your argument

Once you have more or less decided on your attitude to the question (for an answer is never really 'finalised') you have to present your case in the most persuasive manner. In order to do this you must avoid meandering from point to point and instead produce an organised argument — a structured flow of ideas and supporting evidence, leading logically to a conclusion which fully answers the question. Never begin to write until you have produced an outline of your argument.

You may find it easiest to begin by sketching out its main stage as a flow chart or some other form of visual presentation. But eventually you should produce a list of paragraph topics. The paragraph is the conventional written demarcation for a unit of thought and you can outline an argument quite simply by briefly summarising the substance of each paragraph and then checking that these points (you may remember your English teacher referring to them as topic sentences) really do follow a coherent order. Later you will be able to elaborate on each topic, illustrating and qualifying it as you go along. But you will find this far easier to do if you possess from the outset a clear map of where you are heading.

All questions require some form of an argument. Even so-called 'descriptive' questions *imply* the need for an argument. An adequate answer to the request to 'Outline the role of Iago in *Othello*' would do far more than simply list his appearances on stage. It would at the very least attempt to provide some *explanation* for his actions — is he, for example, a representative stage 'Machiavel'? an example of pure evil, 'motiveless malignity'? or a realistic study of a tormented personality reacting to identifiable social and psychological pressures?

Your conclusion ought to address the terms of the question. It may seem obvious, but 'how far do you agree', 'evaluate', 'consider', 'discuss', etc, are *not* interchangeable formulas and your conclusion must take account of the precise wording of the question. If asked 'How far do you agree?', the concluding paragraph of your essay really should state whether you are in complete agreement, total disagreement, or, more likely, partial agreement. Each preceding paragraph should have a clear justification for its existence and help to clarify the reasoning which underlies your conclusion. If you find that a paragraph serves no good purpose (perhaps merely summarising the plot), do not hesitate to discard it.

The arrangement of the paragraphs, the overall strategy of the argument, can vary. One possible pattern is dialectical: present the arguments in favour of one point of view (**thesis**); then turn to counter-arguments or to a rival interpretation (**antithesis**); finally evaluate the competing claims and arrive at your own conclusion (**synthesis**). You may, on the other hand, feel so convinced of the merits of one particular case that you wish to devote your entire essay to arguing that viewpoint persuasively (although it is always desirable to indicate, however briefly, that you are aware of alternative, if flawed, positions). As the essays contained in this volume demonstrate, there are many other possible strategies. Try to adopt the one which will most comfortably accommodate the demands of the question and allow you to express your thoughts with the greatest possible clarity.

Be careful, however, not to apply abstract formulas in a mechanical manner. It is true that you should be careful to define your terms. It is *not* true that every essay should begin with 'The dictionary defines x as . . .'. In fact, definitions are often best left until an appropriate moment for their introduction arrives. Similarly every essay should have a beginning, middle and end. But it does not follow that in your opening paragraph you should announce an intention to write an essay, or that in your concluding paragraph you need to signal an imminent desire to put down your pen. The old adages are often useful reminders of what constitutes good practice, but they must be interpreted intelligently.

Write out the essay

Once you have developed a coherent argument you should aim to communicate it in the most effective manner possible. Make certain you clearly identify yourself, and the question you are answering. Ideally, type your answer, or at least ensure your handwriting is legible and that you leave sufficient space for your tutor's comments. Careless presentation merely distracts from the force of your argument. Errors of grammar, syntax and spelling are far more serious. At best they are an irritating blemish, particularly in the work of a student who should be sensitive to the nuances of language. At worst, they seriously confuse the sense of your argument. If you are aware that you have stylistic problems of this kind, ask your tutor for advice at the earliest opportunity. Everyone, however, is liable to commit the occasional howler. The only remedy is to give yourself plenty of time in which to proof-read your manuscript (often reading it aloud is helpful) before submitting it.

Language, however, is not only an instrument of communication; it is also an instrument of thought. If you want to think clearly and precisely you should strive for a clear, precise prose style. Keep your sentences short and direct. Use modern, straightforward English wherever possible. Avoid repetition, clichés and wordiness. Beware of generalisations, simplifications, and overstatements. Orwell analysed the relationship between stylistic vice and muddled thought in his essay 'Politics and the English Language' (1946) — it remains essential reading (and is still readily available in volume 4 of the Penguin *Collected Essays, Journalism and Letters*). Generalisations, for example, are always dangerous. They are rarely true and tend to suppress the individuality of the texts in question. A remark such as 'Keats always employs sensuous language in his poetry' is not only fatuous (what, after all, does it mean? is *every* word he wrote equally 'sensuous'?) but tends to obscure interesting distinctions which could otherwise be made between, say, the descriptions in the 'Ode on a Grecian Urn' and those in 'To Autumn'.

The intelligent use of quotations can help you make your points with greater clarity. Don't sprinkle them throughout your essay without good reason. There is no need, for example, to use them to support uncontentious statements of fact. 'Macbeth murdered Duncan' does not require textual evidence (unless you wish to dispute Thurber's brilliant parody, 'The Great Macbeth Murder Mystery', which reveals Lady Macbeth's father as the culprit!). Quotations should be included, however, when they are necessary to support your case. The proposition that Macbeth's imaginative powers wither after he has killed his king would certainly require extensive quotation: you would almost certainly want to analyse key passages from both before and after the murder (perhaps his first and last soliloquies?). The key word here is 'analyse'. Quotations cannot make your points on their own. It is up to you to demonstrate their relevance and clearly explain to your readers *why* you want them to focus on the passage you have selected.

Most of the academic conventions which govern the presentation of essays are set out briefly in the style sheet below. The question of gender, however, requires fuller discussion. More than half the population of the world is female. Yet many writers still refer to an undifferentiated *man*kind. Or write of the author and *his* public. We do not think that this convention has much to recommend it. At the very least, it runs the risk of introducing unintended sexist attitudes. And at times leads to such patent absurdities as 'Cleopatra's final speech asserts *man*'s true nobility'. With a little thought, you can normally find ways of expressing yourself which do not suggest that the typical author, critic or reader is male. Often you can simply use plural forms, which is probably a more elegant solution than relying on such awkward formulations as 's/he' or 'he and she'. You should also try to avoid distinguishing between male and female authors on the basis of forenames. Why *Jane* Austen and not *George* Byron? Refer to all authors by their last names unless there is some good reason not to. Where there may otherwise be confusion, say between T S and George Eliot, give the name in full when it first occurs and thereafter use the last name only.

Finally, keep your audience firmly in mind. Tutors and examiners are interested in understanding your conclusions and the processes by which you arrived at them. They are not interested in reading a potted version of a book they already know. **So don't pad out your work with plot summary.**

Hints for examinations

In an examination you should go through exactly the same processes as you would for the preparation of a term essay. The only difference lies in the fact that some of the stages will have had to take place before you enter the examination room. This should not bother you unduly. Examiners are bound to avoid the merely eccentric when they come to formulate papers and if you have read widely and thought deeply about the central issues raised by your set texts you can be confident you will have sufficient material to answer the majority of questions sensibly.

The fact that examinations impose strict time limits makes it *more* rather than less, important that you plan carefully. There really is no point in floundering into an answer without any idea of where you are going, particularly when there will not be time to recover from the initial error.

Before you begin to answer any question at all, study the entire paper with care. Check that you understand the rubric and know how many questions you have to answer and whether any are compulsory. It may be comforting to spot a title you feel confident of answering well, but don't rush to tackle it: read *all* the questions before deciding which *combination* will allow you to display your abilities to the fullest advantage. Once you have made your choice, analyse each question, sketch out your ideas, assemble the evidence, review your initial hypothesis, play your argument, *before* trying to write out an answer. And make notes at each stage: not only will these help you arrive at a sensible conclusion, but examiners are impressed by evidence of careful thought.

Plan your time as well as your answers. If you have practised writing timed essays as part of your revision, you should not find this too difficult. There can be a temptation to allocate extra time to the questions you know you can answer well; but this is always a short-sighted policy. You will find yourself left to face a question which would in any event have given you difficulty without even the time to give it serious thought. It is, moreover, easier to gain marks at the lower end of the scale than at the upper, and you will never compensate for one poor answer by further polishing two satisfactory answers. Try to leave some time at the end of the examination to re-read your answers and correct any obvious errors. If the worst comes to the worst and you run short of time, don't just keep writing until you are forced to break off in mid-paragraph. It is far better to provide for the examiner a set of notes which indicate the overall direction of your argument.

Good luck — but if you prepare for the examination conscientiously and tackle the paper in a methodical manner, you won't need it!

short prose quotation incorporated in the text of the essay, within quotation marks

Verse quotation is indented and introduced by a colon. No quotation marks are needed. The line reference - in brackets - follows the quotation.

His letters in the later part of this year are full of his consciousness of his dying younger brother: 'His identity presses upon me so all day that I am obliged to go out . . . I am obliged to write, and plunge into abstract images to ease myself of his countenance his voice his feebleness'.

Keats's poetry was always aware of mortality. In 'Sleep and Poetry' he knows:

> life is but a day;
> A fragile dew-drop on its perilous way
> From a tree's summit
>
> (ll.85–87)

and that the time when he can 'sleep in the grass' and 'Feed on apples red, and strawberries', will given way to 'a nobler life' where he 'may find the agonies, the strife/ Of human hearts'. In this poem he examines the nature of poetry and sees clearly that to dwell too long on the 'burrs,/ And thorns of life' is to distort the truth. The Gothic — 'trees uptorn/ Darkness, and worms, and shrouds, and sepulchres', as we know from 'Isabella' and from 'La Belle Dame sans Merci', had its attraction for Keats, as it had for his contemporaries. After the fashion of Leigh Hunt,[1] he knew it to be as unhealthy for the imagination as an over-indulgence in sweets. Keats conceived the function of poetry and the role of the poet in the terms of the calling to which he was first apprenticed: medicine. He sees the poet as healer, poetry as health-giving. The great end of poetry, he says, in 'Sleep and Poetry' — anticipating the 'Ode on a Grecian Urn' — is to be:

> . . . a friend
> To sooth the cares and lift the thoughts of man.
>
> (ll.246–247)

short verse quotation incorporated in the text of the essay, within quotation marks. Line endings are indicated by a slash (/).

ication of footnote

poem titles in quotation marks.

Three dots (ellipsis) indicate where words or phrases have been cut from a quotation, and are normally also used (as here) when a quotation begins mid-sentence.

'The Fall of Hyperion' Keats still uses these terms:

> . . . sure a poet is a sage;
> A humanist, Physician to all men.
>
> (ll.189–190)

---

[1] Leight Hunt, 1784–1859, essayist and poet. Keats's first published poem appeared in Hunt's journal, *The Examiner*, and his very early work was influenced by Hunt's style.

footnote

Line references should normally be given in assignment essays and in examination essays where a text is supplied.

title of literary journal in italics. In a handwritten or typed manuscript this would appear as underlining: The Examiner.

We have divided the following information into two sections. Part A describes those rules which it is essential to master no matter what kind of essay you are writing (including examination answers). Part B sets out some of the more detailed conventions which govern the documentation of essays.

PART A: LAYOUT

Titles of texts

Titles of published books, plays (of any length), long poems, pamphlets and periodicals (including newspapers and magazines), works of classical literature, and films should be underlined: e.g. David Copperfield (novel), Twelfth Night (play), Paradise Lost (long poem), Critical Quarterly (periodical), Horace's Ars Poetica (Classical work), Apocalypse Now (film).

Notice how important it is to distinguish between titles and other names. Hamlet is the play; Hamlet the prince. Wuthering Heights is the novel; Wuthering Heights the house. Underlining is the equivalent in handwritten or typed manuscripts of printed italics. So what normally appears in this volume as *Othello* would be written as Othello in your essay.

Titles of articles, essays, short stories, short poems, songs, chapters of books, speeches, and newspaper articles are enclosed in quotation marks; e.g. 'The Flea' (short poem), 'The Prussian Officer' (short story), 'Middleton's Chess Strategies' (article), 'Thatcher Defects!' (newspaper headline).

Exceptions: Underlining titles or placing them within quotation marks does not apply to sacred writings (e.g. Bible, Koran, Old Testament, Gospels) or parts of a book (e.g. Preface, Introduction, Appendix).

It is generally incorrect to place quotation marks around a title of a published book which you have underlined. The exception is 'titles within titles': e.g. 'Vanity Fair: A Critical Study (title of a book about *Vanity Fair*).

Quotations

Short verse quotations of a single line or part of a line should be incorporated within quotation marks as part of the running text of your essay. Quotations of two or three lines of verse are treated in the same way, with line endings indicated by a slash(/). For example:

1 In <u>Julius Caesar</u>, Antony says of Brutus, 'This was the noblest Roman of them all'.
2 The opening of Antony's famous funeral oration, 'Friends, Romans, Countrymen, lend me your ears;/ I come to bury Caesar not to praise him', is a carefully controlled piece of rhetoric.

Longer verse quotations of more than three lines should be indented from the main body of the text and introduced in most cases with a colon. Do not enclose indented quotations within quotation marks. For example:

It is worth pausing to consider the reasons Brutus gives to justify his decision to assassinate Caesar:

> It must be by his death; and for my part,
> I know no personal cause to spurn at him,
> But for the general. He would be crowned.
> How might that change his nature, there's the question.

At first glance his rationale may appear logical . . .

Prose quotations of less than three lines should be incorporated in the text of the essay, within quotation marks. Longer prose quotations should be indented and the quotation marks omitted. For example:

1 Before his downfall, Caesar rules with an iron hand. His political opponents, the Tribunes Marullus and Flavius, are 'put to silence' for the trivial offence of 'pulling scarfs off Caesar's image'.
2 It is interesting to note the rhetorical structure of Brutus's Forum speech:

> Romans, countrymen, and lovers, hear me for my cause, and be silent that you may hear. Believe me for my honour, and have respect to mine honour that you may believe. Censure me in your wisdom, and awake your senses, that you may the better judge.

Tenses: When you are relating the events that occur within a work of fiction or describing the author's technique, it is the convention to use the present tense. Even though Orwell published *Animal Farm* in 1945, the book *describes* the animals' seizure of Manor Farm. Similarly, Macbeth always *murders* Duncan, despite the passage of time.

PART B: DOCUMENTATION

When quoting from verse of more than twenty lines, provide line references: e.g. In 'Upon Appleton House' Marvell's mower moves 'With whistling scythe and elbow strong' (1.393).

Quotations from plays should be identified by act, scene and line references: e.g. Prospero, in Shakespeare's The Tempest, refers to Caliban as 'A devil, a born devil' (IV.1.188). (i.e. Act 4. Scene 1. Line 188).

Quotations from prose works should provide a chapter reference and, where appropriate, a page reference.

Bibliographies should list full details of all sources consulted. The way is which they are presented varies, but one standard format is as follows:

1 Books and articles are listed in alphabetical order by the author's last name. Initials are placed after the surname.
2 If you are referring to a chapter or article within a larger work, you list it by reference to the author of the article or chapter, not the editor (although the editor is also named in the reference).
3 Give (in parentheses) the place and date of publication, e.g. (London, 1962). These details can be found within the book itself. Here are some examples:

   Brockbank, J. P., 'Shakespeare's Histories, English and Roman', in Ricks, C. (ed.) English Drama to 1710 (Sphere History of Literature in the English Language) (London, 1971).
   Gurr, A., 'Richard III and the Democratic Process', Essays in Criticism 24 (1974), pp. 39–47.
   Spivack, B., Shakespeare and the Allegory of Evil (New York, 1958).

Footnotes: In general, try to avoid using footnotes and build your references into the body of the essay wherever possible. When you do use them give the full bibliographic reference to a work in the first instance and then use a short title: e.g. See K. Smidt, <u>Unconformities in Shakespeare's History Plays</u> (London, 1982), pp. 43–47 becomes Smidt (pp. 43–47) thereafter. Do not use terms such as 'ibid.' or 'op. cit.' unless you are absolutely sure of their meaning.

There is a principle behind all this seeming pedantry. The reader ought to be able to find and check your references and quotations as quickly and easily as possible. Give additional information, such as canto or volume number whenever you think it will assist your reader.

SUGGESTIONS FOR FURTHER READING

Texts
These essays have, where possible, followed *Selected Poems & Letters of Keats*, ed. R Gittings (London, 1966), since this edition is so frequently prescribed for students. The following, however, offer a fuller range of material:

Barnard, J (ed.), *John Keats: The Complete Poems* (Harmondsworth, 1973)

Gittings, R (ed.), *The Letters of John Keats* (Oxford, 1970).

Biography
Gittings, R, *John Keats* (London, 1968; Harmondsworth, 1971)

General studies
Barnard, J, *John Keats* (Cambridge, 1987)

Ricks, C, *Keats and Embarrassment* (Oxford, 1984)

Walsh, W, *Introduction to Keats* (London, 1981)

Watts, C, *Preface to Keats* (Harlow, 1985)

Essay collections
Fraser, G S (ed.), *Keats: Odes* (Macmillan Casebook, 1971)

Hill, J S (ed.), *Keats: Narrative Poems* (Macmillan Casebook, 1983)

Muir, K (ed.), *John Keats: A Reassessment* (Liverpool, 1958)

Longman Group UK Limited
*Longman House, Burnt Mill, Harlow, Essex, CM20 2JE, England
and Associated Companies throughout the World.*

© Longman Group UK Limited 1988

First published 1988
ISBN 0 582 00652 X

*Set in 10/12 pt Century Schoolbook, Linotron 202
Printed in Great Britain by Bell and Bain Ltd., Glasgow*

Acknowledgement
The editors would like to thank Zachary Leader for his assist-
ance with the style sheet.